Advance Praise for Overcomers, Inc.

"I travel the world teaching about diversity and empowerment, and how we can all rise above our own personal circumstances and become better people. When I read *Overcomers, Inc.*, I was struck by the diversity of the authors and their stories, yet the book comes together around a strong message: that no situation is hopeless, that no one is ever alone, and that everyone can reach beyond their circumstances and triumph. This is a book for everyone. It will empower and uplift all who read it. Highly recommended."

~ **Dr. Maura Cullen,**
Leading Diversity Speaker,
author of *35 Dumb Things Well-Intended People Say*,
www.TheDiversitySpeaker.com

"One of my favorite sayings is 'The only way out is through!' This wonderful book is full of stories about people who didn't let fear, pain, or discouragement stop them from pursuing their paths. Very inspiring and highly recommended!"

~ **Dale Goldstein, LCSW,**
author of the award-winning book, *Heartwork: How To Get What You Really, REALLY Want*,
www.AwakenTheHeart.org

"Life is always a series of challenges. Some small - some beyond challenging. And as this book so beautifully promises, always there is hope. So expect to be inspired and uplifted by these real life stories of triumph and spiritual expansion. And it's a good read!"

~ **Judith Sherven, PhD, and Jim Sniechowski, PhD,**
authors of #1 best seller *The Heart of Marketing*,
www.JudithandJim.com

"The stories in this book are not only inspiring, they are also thought provoking. They make you look at your life and want to do more and be more. They provide both hope and optimism and give you a sense that you can truly accomplish anything."

~ **Kimberly A. Mylls,**
co-author of *Boys Before Business:*
The Single Girl's Guide to Having it All,
co-founder of www.DearGodLetter.com

"A seriously terrific book. I was moved to tears and laughter within pages, and can't wait to order a box to give as gifts. *Overcomers, Inc.* also happens to be a genuine reflection of the humanity of the authors. Both book and authors are wise, light, and make the world a better place."

~ **Andrea J. Lee,**
author, *How I Wonder...Thought Leadership in a Noisy World,*
www.AndreaJLee.com

It is no coincidence that happiness, gratitude in practice, and simple yet time-honored truths are key themes in this beautiful collection of stories where faith, hope, optimism, and sheer determination triumph over the worst of odds. If you're stuck in a rut, or doing well, either way you'll enjoy the unfailingly positive message and relish the tools *Overcomers, Inc.* provides to surface deep gratitude and awareness to empower your life."

~ **Maryam Webster,**
author, *Everyday Bliss For Busy Women*

There is no better way to work on your life than to have a coach or mentor beside you helping you keep your eye on the goal and cheering you on. The stories in *Overcomers, Inc.* inspire you to reach deeper and work harder, knowing that it is possible to rise above disappointments, set-backs, and tragedies, to succeed and become the best you can possibly be.

~ **Ruth Lee,**
author of *Angel of the Maya,*
www.MeditateWithRuthLee.com

"*Overcomers, Inc.* is filled with inspirational stories from ordinary people who faced extraordinary challenges and overcame them through persistence and hard work. No matter where you are in life, they will inspire you to even greater accomplishment. Buy it, read it, live it.

~ **Lee Pound,**
editor, publisher, coach,
author of *57 Steps to Better Writing*

"As a firm believer that we have complete control over how we graciously accept the lessons of life, I am refreshed through reading *Overcomers, Inc.* This body of work chronicles the ultimate journey of acceptance and opportunity. If you've ever found yourself questioning "why?" something happened, you must read this book. The stories reinforce that there is always a "how" that will move you on to the next delicious experience in life. We may not always know the reason something happens when it's happening, but we can always apply the lesson to enrich our lives."

~ **Lisa Manyon,**
Professional Copywriting & Marketing Strategist,
www.LisaManyon.com

"At a time in the world when so many people are feeling fear about their future and questioning their faith, *Overcomers, Inc.* comes as a Divine answer, reminding us that when faced with what seems to be insurmountable odds, miracles occur when we approach life with a loving, open and courageous heart. After reading each story, you cannot help being transformed in some way. This is one book you'll keep by your nightstand for when you need a dose of hope and inspiration!"

~ **Lorraine Cohen,**
Spiritual Life Coach & Advisor, Speaker, Broadcaster,
www.Powerfull-Living.biz

"These true stories of regular people overcoming tough times will give you the strength to carry on to the peace and healing possible in your own life. Each one is a jewel of inspiration and encouragement."

~ **Art Maines, LCSW**

"These pieces will make you want to cry and smile at the same time. They are heart-wrenching, inspiring, and right from the heart. If you're going through a tough time and need inspiration, the words in *Overcomers, Inc.* will remind you that you're not alone. The authors remind us that even in the midst of terrible change and crisis, hope and transformation are not only possible but inevitable."

~ Anna Stookey, MA, MFT,
Bodymind Specialist and Psychotherapist,
www.AnnaStookey.com

"Fans of our film "You" are often looking for comforting ways to overcome the loss the film depicts. I found the book magnificent. To read these stories of people who have 'overcome' throws such light on my own process. I found it enlightening, very useful and I highly recommend it."

~Gildart Jackson,
producer, writer, actor,
www.YOUTHEFILM.com

"At the end of reading the beautiful poignant stories, the first word that came to my mind was "Wow!" These are extraordinary and brave stories....not only inspiring, but soul stirring. Each one of these narratives is proof that there is a choice to co-create with Source that will inevitably bring healing. All the authors had the trust, willingness, and courage to make that choice, and surrender to the mystery of life's unfolding, demonstrating how tragedies, illness, disappointment and betrayal can be shape-shifted into miracles. It is a noble book not only for these unprecedented turbulent times, and serves as a beacon of hope for all of us in the human condition."

~ Max Wellspring,
www.TheWellSpringSolution.com

"I was moved to tears by the inspiring stories of *Overcomers, Inc.* My heart filled with renewed faith in the miraculous strength and resilien cy of the human spirit."

~ Cindy Morris, MSW.
Best-selling author of *Priestess Entrepreneur: Success is an Inside Job*,
www.PracticalPriestess.com

"If you need a quick dose of encouragement, the wisdom you will read here will help you learn to embrace tragedy, deal with it quickly and be thankful for it, instead of considering it the bane of society. When you finish reading this marvelous collection of stories, thank God for His grace in your life. Then pass this copy on to the person who needs it most. You'll know who it is."

~Rhea Perry,
Educator for Families and Entrepreneurs,
www.RheaPerry.com

"Wow! I was so touched and moved by the stories in *Overcomers, Inc.*! I love reading stories that inspire me - and this book definitely delivers. *Overcomers, Inc.* will not only inspire you, it will empower you, granting not only hope, but the tenacity and courage to never give up, never stop believing, and always keep moving forward. I **highly** recommend it!"

~ Hallie Thompson,
www.EnlightenedHopeBook.com

"At a time in our culture when there is such a media focus on the negative, this book is a refreshing blessing. This book has three gifts to share with the reader. First, it serves as a source of inspiration to help us overcome our own challenges. Second, the contributing authors are real life role models in "how to" overcome. Third, and I think this may be the most subtle yet important gift, it gives us a broader perspective about the true magnitude of our own challenges. Using *Overcomers, Inc.* as a kind of benchmark, we can ask ourselves, "Is what is happening to me right now really as bad as I'm making it out to be?" Thank you for your vision and bringing all of these amazing people together so they could share their stories."

~ Kelly LeFevre, MSM, LMT,
author, Speaker & Marketing Coach,
www.MassageandProsper.com

"*Overcomers, Inc.* is an inspiring, heart-focused book of real-life stories about individuals with real-life challenges; ones we all have to find ways to overcome every day. I found it comforting to read, to know 'I'm not alone' in my own challenges. Everyone has them and some unfortunately much larger than mine. I also found it heartwarming to read that those with so many obstacles in life chose to make such a huge difference in others' lives in return, and in doing so became heroes themselves."

~ **Katrina Sawa,**
The JumpStart Your Biz Coach,
www.JumpStartYourMarketing.com

"Before you read *Overcomers, Inc.*, start your engines of courage, faith, and strength. You will need them to keep up with the incredible authors who wrote and lived these stories. These stories of hope demonstrate that you always have a choice between victimhood and triumph. This is a book that everyone must read, study, and practice. Then, never let anything stop you again!"

~ **Jimm Hughey, MS,**
Master Wealth Acceleration Coach,
www.LoveandMoneyforCouples.com

"This book is an amazing compilation of inspiring, uplifting, and motivating stories that will keep you wanting more! After reading these heartfelt stories, I feel enlightened and empowered to deal with adversity from an entirely different perspective! Thank you to all the brave authors who shared their stories!"

~ **Jana Hollingsworth,**
Intuitive Life Coach,
www.JanaHollingsworth.com

"*Overcomers Inc.* is the text for the College of Hard Knocks. Taking responsibility against all odds is the lesson these authors teach us through their experiences. Life can be easy and we can handle anything."

~**Dr. Rich Jones**

"*Overcomers, Inc.* crosses all borders of life. It doesn't matter where you live, the color of your skin, or the state of your physical health. There are times when life throws you a curve ball and you feel all alone. *Overcomers, Inc.* is your companion during those tough times. Reading these stories will inspire you and offer you hope - hope that you'll overcome your tough time in life. This is one of those books I strongly recommend to all my patients."

~ **Dr. Michael Kaye,**
www.DrMichaelKaye.com

"Reading through the stories in *Overcomers, Inc.*, I find there are people just like me, facing similar challenges in life, who have found ways to overcome their problems and find the opportunities to grow and be more than they were before.

Filled with good common sense advice and written in a friendly way, drawing me into each story, this book should be a good read for many seekers like myself, who want to have something to read, that they can dip in and out of, to strengthen their days."

~ **Stephen J. Robin,**
Seminarian and CCO,
www.solutionsnotproblems.com

"*Overcomers, Inc.* is an eminently readable series of true tales, written by people of all ages and backgrounds. All have confronted adversity in one form or another and prevailed. While deceptively simple, this volume contains deep truths about how to rise above calamity, seeing the good instead of the bad, maintaining hope despite despair, and recognizing that gratitude and forgiveness are truly empowering. Read this book! You will not only enjoy it, but will find yourself empowered to go beyond some crushing realities which hold you down or bring you low. These tales, depicting the impact of faith in God's goodness, coupled with a belief in one's innate human resilience, will inspire you and enable you to overcome perennial overwhelm. Instead, these memorable, heartwarming vignettes will help you attain your dreams in ways you never thought possible."

~**Rabbi Ed Weinsberg, Ed.D., D.D.**
Author of *Conquer Prostate Cancer: How Medicine,
Faith, Love and Sex Can Renew Your Life,*
www.ConquerProstateCancer.com

OVERCOMERS,

INC.

True Stories of Hope, Courage and Inspiration

Compiled by

LYNNE KLIPPEL

Love Your Life

Love Your Life Publishing, Inc.

Love Your Life Publishing, Inc.
7127 Mexico Road, Suite 121
Saint Peters, MO 63376
800-930-6430

ISBN: 978-1-934509-26-5
Library of Congress Control Number: 2009908265

Printed simultaneously in the United States of America and Canada.

Cover and internal design: Sarah Barrie, www.Cyanotype.ca
Editing: Marlene Oulton, www.BulletProofers.com

TABLE OF CONTENTS

Section 1- Hope

Section 2- Courage

Acknowledgements

This book is a miracle and the result of the labors of many hands and hearts. First, thank you to the authors who each contributed a chapter to this book. Your willingness to share your story so that others would be uplifted is remarkable and rare. Thank you for your honesty, enthusiasm, and for being a light to the world. It is an honor to have your story in this book.

The team who worked behind the scenes to produce this book did a remarkable job. Thank you for Marlene Oulton for editing and polishing each story, to Tomar Levine for outstanding proof-reading, to Sarah Barrie for her lovely design, and to Kathleen Gage and her team for creating a marketing plan as unique as the book. We see you as our book angels who deserve a ticker-tape parade for your work on this project.

Ruth Lee, Leni Onkka, and Christine Kloser provided moral and spiritual support for this project. The book would not have been published without you. Thank you for your wisdom and unstinting support. You are treasured friends and mentors.

All of the authors wish to thank our loved ones for giving us time and space to write, for reading our sample chapters, and for believing in our message. You are our inspiration!

Most importantly, we thank you, our readers. We hope that you are blessed and uplifted by the stories in this book.

Dedication

This book is dedicated to everyone who has ever suffered, worried, or cried in the night. You are not alone.

And, especially for
Roland, Shirley, and David who live as Overcomers
every day.

We deem those happy who from the experience of life have learnt to bear its ills without being overcome by them.

~ CARL JUNG

Introduction

At one point in my life it seemed like everywhere I looked, I saw tragedy. My brother, both of my parents, and a dear friend were all battling cancer at the same time. Other friends were losing jobs and fearful about the prospects of finding new work. The evening news was full of financial scandals, plant closings, kidnappings, and war.

As I sat in the sun on my front porch in March 2009, I wished I had a book to send to my brother to read during his chemotherapy treatments - something to remind him that he was not alone and to encourage him to fight for his life. I wanted a book that could give him hope, inspiration, and encouragement on every page.

Due to a series of miracles, the book you are now reading is my wish come true. In a very short time a team of wonderful people came together to create this book with just one purpose: to encourage you, the reader, to overcome whatever obstacles are lying in your path to happiness.

As you read the stories in this book, you will find real life tales of remarkable courage, strength, and perseverance. You will be inspired, entertained, and uplifted. Some of the stories will make you laugh. Some of them will make you cry. All of them will make you proud of the power of the human spirit.

You will find this a book of diversity. There are many authors, from many walks of life. However, they all share a common bond. They triumphed over tragedy and gleaned wisdom in this process. While this is not a religious book, these are stories full of faith, of many kinds and flavors. It is funny how in your darkest times, faith often becomes your brightest light.

All of the contributors to this book want to encourage you to hold tight to your belief that a better day will come. It is their sincere desire to pass along what they've learned through their own trials, to make your journey easier.

I hope that you wear this book out by highlighting meaningful passages and bending down the corners of the pages you want to read over and over again. There is true wisdom in these pages that can help you feel strong, brave, and hopeful.

May you be blessed by this book and inspired to overcome!

Lynne Klippel
St. Peters, Missouri
September, 2009

HOPE

Hope begins in the dark, the stubborn hope that if you just show up
and try to do the right thing, the dawn will come.
You wait and watch and work: You don't give up.
~ Anne Lamott

When Tough Times Hit, There Is Always HOPE!

Mary Hays-Bridges

"Mary, they're calling for you in surgery." It seemed as if I was stuck in the black hole of a revolving door to the operating room. My well-written plan of action for my life was now an empty sheet, and there was nothing that I could do to stop the impending implosion. I knew that focusing on the "why" or the "if only" was wasted energy, but the empty numbness I felt couldn't stop the "what just happened" questions from bombarding my conscious thoughts. To make the torment worse, I had been admitted to the pediatric ward of the hospital, which was a tough pill to swallow for a 20 year old cadet. Coming to consciousness, I realized that apparently I now seemed to have a 6 year old "buddy" using his artistic talent and crayons to draw new highways for his toy cars, using my full-leg cast as his medium.

Since age five I dreamed of becoming an astronaut. Suddenly fatherless at age twelve, I prayed for a Father to help me to become an astronaut and teach me about life. I asked for one - two were sent: Col. James B. Irwin, (Apollo 15 – 8th man on the moon), to be my mentor, and Dr. Robert H. Schuller, (*Hour of Power* TV program), to be my possibility thinking coach.

A pilot's license before I learned to drive a car, appointments to West Point and the United States Air Force Academy, (entered USAFA in one of the first classes of women), with NASA in sight was just the beginning.

While a cadet, I had an orthopedic sports injury. Treatment by a famous civilian surgeon included a full leg cast and medicine - given improperly off label. (The FDA withdrew the drug from the market seven months later). The knowledge that the doctor's judgment had been impaired by a brain tumor came too late. I was fighting for my life with multiple, life-threatening drug complications: catastrophic immune-suppression, chemically induced diabetes and lupus, a perforated stomach, kidney stones, shingles, swelling in the brain – on top of my leg and spine injuries. Everyday a new specialist – an added diagnosis – to the point of my main Internist asking, "Mary, why are you still alive?" I wondered myself.

I was facing something more difficult than trying to survive the devastation from a negligent act. I had truly lost my sense of identity, purpose, and life goals. I could survive being a helpless invalid, but to be hopeless would be downright tragic.

Everyday, my "Moon Dad," as Jim liked me to call him, visited me in the hospital. One afternoon he was especially somber, tearfully telling me that the doors were closed to my flying. The Academy and NASA – everything I had worked so hard for - all the eggs in my basket were now gone.

Sitting at my hospital bedside, he quietly began sharing his personal moon journey. He made sights and sounds come alive with the technical jargon. As the moon landing approached, he placed my hand, IV's and all, on the joystick (THE control unit from Apollo 15 Lunar Module Falcon), brought back from the moon. His hand over mine, we made "my" moon landing. With a tearful closure, we grieved and laid to rest what truly had been "our" moon dream.

The next visit he asked what my new dream would be. "I want to get well." "Not big enough," he responded. The next day, he asked again. "I want to get well and to walk." "Not big enough." As my condition worsened, this daily banter continued. I could do nothing more than watch the seasons change while enjoying the spectacular view of Pikes Peak out my window. It's easy to hope in good times, but it's a whole different ballgame learning how to hope during tough challenges.

Praying for a new dream, I searched my heart for a meaningful goal that would give me a sense of purpose and bring an exciting new dimension to life. It was not a time to give up, but to give in to a new dream, a time to refocus, stay grounded, and start life over. The challenge would be to commit to a new dream despite my disabilities.

I could have remained a grump, but Kevin, (aka six year-old leg cast artist), taught me a powerful lesson - to view life through the happy, joyful eyes of a child. Many mornings I heard him running down the hospital hallway to my room, the little feet on his too-big, one piece pajamas flapping on the hard floor announcing his arrival. With his precious lisp, he recited, "Maawy, this is the day that the Lord has made. Let us "wejoice" and be glad!" What a lesson in optimism from a tyke who was profoundly ill.

Once again to Irwin's question, I responded, "I'm going to get well, get in shape, become a runner, AND... run to the top of that mountain." Looking at the snow-covered Pikes Peak in the distance, he paused for a long time. Turning to me, he smiled, "Now that's what I'm talking about! That's big enough to keep hope alive." My Pikes Peak journey had begun.

"When faced with a mountain – I WILL NOT QUIT! I will keep on striving until I climb over, find a pass through, tunnel underneath, or simply stay and turn the mountain into a gold mine." - Dr. Robert H. Schuller.

I began writing my new definition of HOPE:

H-appiness
O-ptimism
P-erseverance through Positive Possibilities
E-ndurance

To keep HOPE alive, I learned that:

- When one door closes, believe that God will put a brand new dream in your heart. He will open doors no one can shut. It's up to us to step up to the starting line to run a new race.

- Great things happen when you gather the courage to take that step and face your mountain!

- Positive attitude, thoughts and self-talk are ingredients that go into the recipe of life that, when baked in the trials of this world, will bring forth happiness.

- We are never given more difficulties than we can handle. Learning to smile while enduring a challenge can springboard to a more mature faith.

- Life is not a sprint, but a lengthy, challenging marathon fraught with hills and unnumbered difficulties. Prepare for the distance.

- The only true "disability" is one we impose on ourselves. Infinite possibilities are ours! It is promised to us! (Phil 4:13: "I can do everything through Him...") All possibility thinkers are called to greatness, even if it's from a hospital bed!

- At moments when you think you can't take any more, you'll be blessed with new resources of strength, courage, and commitment. Subsequent growth empowers you with momentum.

- Joy is the by-product of HOPE.

- True survival has little to do with any power within ourselves. It is all about the sustained, powerful presence of God in our life. Jesus is the anchor of HOPE!

That first year in the hospital proved foundational, grounding me in HOPE for the subsequent life challenges in my battle to survive. In the ensuing thirty years, my healing necessitated a total of four years of accumulated hospital time, twenty years of crutches, leg braces, wheel-chairs and fifty-seven surgeries (the last surgery, a front/back spinal fusion at L4-S1 with cages/rods/bolts).

Twenty years post-Academy injury, I stood with other runners, successfully taking on Pikes Peak – the toughest race on the North American continent. Getting to this point had been a journey of bless-ings. The 14,110' summit seemed intimidating, but I approached the mountain in the same way that I had each challenge along the way – one step at a time.......with HOPE!

My job in life now is to help others set new dreams and learn about survival – through Him. May my story impress upon you that HOPE can bring you through life's trials! Dreams DO come true! All things ARE possible! As a coach, "HOPE" now has added meaning for me - "**H**elping **O**thers' **P**ossibilities **E**ndure."

- Before going to sleep, answer: "Today has been a good day because
  _____." Focus on the people you love, the things that inspire you, the daily details that are within your power to change. Happiness is found in these small details of life.

- Keep a goals/gratitude journal. Today, what action step did you take towards your goal? Focusing on goals gives a renewed sense of purpose, adds confidence, cultivates self-esteem, and adds structure to life. Writing down your action steps and daily progress is a positive reinforcement. Counting your blessings adds a measure of humility, compassion and keeps optimism alive.

- Read and/or listen to motivational and inspirational books.

Use pictures and sayings to make a focus board collage for each goal. Seeing these positive affirmations daily enhances your endurance and strength. Become your own cheerleader through positive self-talk.

Happiness + Optimism + Perseverance + Endurance = HOPE

When tough times hit, never give up HOPE!

Specialty certified Health/Wellness Coach **Mary Hays-Bridges** *champions others in their dreams. Her story and song were heard worldwide on* Hour of Power. *She received Dr. Robert H. Schuller's, "Scars to Stars" Possibility Thinkers Award and serves as a Crystal Cathedral ministering Lead Elder. Part-owners of Alaska Open Imaging Center, she and husband, Dr. Bob, call Alaska and California home. A website/book about her Pikes Peak journey are forthcoming. Contact her by email at MaryHaysBridges@yahoo.com.*

Coincidence is God's Way of Remaining Anonymous

Martha-Lee Bohn

Hurricane Katrina. For most people, these words conjure images of desperation, flood waters, and incompetence. For thousands of others, however, Hurricane Katrina is a story of hope and Divine inspiration

Within days of the storm, trucks loaded with chain saws, generators and water arrived from Presbyterian Disaster Assistance. Churches became disaster recovery centers without the benefit of committees examining the problem and deciding what to do.

As Director of Youth Ministries at my local church, the teenagers, who were out of school for six weeks after "the Storm," hung out with me at the church. We were there when volunteers started showing up with tools and supplies, offering help. We became "camp hosts" for the church, dispatching volunteers to help families "muck out" their homes.

Months after the storm, volunteers were sent to the home of an elderly couple. Debris piles were everywhere. Street signs were down, fabric hung from trees, empty neighborhoods. Their house was a mess with moldy furniture, wet sheetrock, and debris.

The couple had managed to clear a space in the kitchen and set up a sleeping pallet in there. The volunteers went to work. They swept out the mess, cut the sheetrock, hauled trash, and jury-rigged the kitchen sink and counter.

When they were done, the old man said, "You have no idea what you have just done for us." The volunteer team leader said, "You would have done it for me. God loves you. It is my blessing to be able to help you."

The old man said, "You don't understand. You are the first people to visit us since the storm. No one has checked on us. My wife and I had become so desperate that we'd made a pact to commit suicide tomorrow, and then you showed up."

Stunned, the volunteer leader said, "I have a work order here. Someone must have spoken with you. We were sent here." Looking at the work order, the old man said, "That's not my house. That's the house on the next street." Yup. It's clear. Someone sent them there. And God keeps sending volunteers to help.

As Outreach Coordinator for the Presbytery of Mississippi Disaster Recovery, I travel the country visiting churches that have sent mission teams to the Gulf Coast. I share stories of hope out of chaos and thank them for "loving their neighbor as themselves."

However, if you had told me years ago that one day I would live in Mississippi and travel around to churches delivering sermons and studies, I would have laughed. Me?

"And further," you tell me, "You will return to your home town a witness to God's hope and presence in the chaos of hurricane recovery and in your own life."

Please. You must be joking. I was raised Presbyterian in suburban New York. We're supposed to be "God's Frozen Chosen." We don't evangelize or talk about religion, much less "witness," whatever that means. And Mississippi? Why would I ever want to live in Mississippi?

And then, a man asked me to marry him. We met at the First International Laughter Symposium in Orlando, Florida in May. I was there presenting a film, "Praise Ha!" about the healing power of laughter. He was a retired Navy nurse who had been to Clown School and was an aspiring stand-up comedian.

During the question and answer period after the film, this man, wearing a chicken hat, stood up, and asked me to marry him. At lunch he told me he was serious and presented me with a ring, an onion ring.

He "courted" me long-distance with letters, flowers and care packages. In spite of my mother's concern that he was Jack the Ripper, I agreed to travel with him to festivals and stand-up comedy clubs that summer. Not only didn't we kill each other, we fell in love. By October, we were engaged.

Moving to south Mississippi, I discovered the third coast of the United States, a whole new world. Firmly in the "Bible Belt," the best way to find community in Mississippi is through church, so I sought out a Presbyterian one. We became regulars at worship and church suppers and hung out with the teenage youth group.

A year later, Matt and I were married at my home church in New York. When we went in for the final kiss, he pulled a clown nose out of his pocket and we were presented as clown and wife! Meeting Matt, taking a leap of faith, falling in love, getting married - it was an exciting whirlwind. I was floating on happiness. It was like a fairy tale.

The fairy tale abruptly ended on my wedding night when my new husband, unexpectedly, tragically, suffered a massive heart attack and died. He was dead before the ambulance even arrived. Twelve hours from bride to widow. It was surreal. "Oh God!" I thought. "How could you do this to me? What happened?!"

What happened? I walked through the valley of the shadow of death and was cared for. God sent angels. Family and friends were glimmers of light in the darkness. Everyone at the wedding walked through it with me. My sisters helped me return to Mississippi. Friends flew in and stayed with me.

That winter and spring, I waded through probate of Matt's Will and worked on "one big thing a day." Sometimes, that big thing was to take a shower or to fix a meal. Wednesday suppers and Sunday worship became my social outings of the week.

By summer I could make it through a week without crying. I spent July and August with family and friends and dared to think about a new future. Coming to terms with the fact that people die, I still wondered aloud, "Why Mississippi? What am I going to do in Mississippi?"

The church asked me to serve as Interim Director of Youth Ministries beginning Labor Day weekend. I agreed and prepared to head south from Seattle. Before I even started packing the car, Hurricane Katrina roared into the Gulf of Mexico. I watched in horror, recognizing places on the Weather Channel!

The first email I received about my house came from a neighbor's cousin saying that my house was "still standing." Driving home from Seattle I kept checking my email and trying to reach anyone by phone. A second email with a first-hand account from my neighbor said, "There is water still coming out of your house." When a church friend sent a text message, "Come home. We'll help you." I realized that Mississippi was now home.

After months of wrestling with grief and arguing with God, Hurricane Katrina turned out to be something of a blessing to me. I found truth in a Bible passage from Romans 5:3-5, "...we also boast in our sufferings, knowing that suffering produces endurance, and endurance produces character, and character produces hope, and hope does not disappoint us."

Thousands of people were suffering. I could no longer allow myself the "luxury" of wallowing in self-pity when I have unique skills and abilities to offer in the midst of chaos. I realized that I didn't die when my husband did. I found my purpose. I decided that God brought me to Mississippi for a reason, and I'd better get to work.

With that decision everything changed. Family and friends saw a young widow facing one more impossible tragedy. I saw a calling, a homework assignment from God.

Mother Theresa once said, "God only gives us as much as we can handle. I just wish He didn't have so much confidence in me." Well, He does have a great deal of confidence in all of us, and with the help of angels disguised as ordinary humans, we can all live in that confidence.

Believe in miracles and be willing to receive the gifts that are offered.

When a volunteer asked me one Sunday night, "What should I do with the hundred pair of shoes I have in the car?" I didn't know what to say. Overwhelmed with a long list of things to do, I said nothing, hoping he was pulling my leg. When he repeated it, saying that they were brand new children's shoes, I knew he was serious.

I called a church member who is an elementary school teacher and told her about the shoes. She responded, "Oh my God, Martha-Lee. You are an answer to prayers. I've been sitting here praying for shoes!"

Working at a low-income elementary school, she manages the "clothing closet" donations for the kids. On Friday, a barefoot boy had come to her asking for shoes. She had no shoes, but she promised him she'd have a pair for him on Monday. It was Sunday night, and she had no shoes for him. I told her to please stop praying!

Consider when something feels like an unexpected burden, it may just be that God is using you to answer someone's prayers! Choose to believe that coincidence is God's way of remaining anonymous.

Originally a New Yorker, **Martha-Lee Bohn** *moved to Mississippi in 2003 after she met a man, fell in love, and got married. Her Gulfport home flooded like thousands of others along the Gulf Coast. Bohn works with Presbyterian Disaster Assistance in the wake of the 2005 Hurricane season. Four years since Katrina, volunteers continue to help families who have lost hope. For more information or to offer help, contact Mississippi InterFaith Disaster Task Force www.msidtf.org.*

One Size Does Not Fit All

Nancie Benson

I was 100 pounds overweight and had reached the point where I absolutely could not start another diet, no matter how much I wanted to. I tried starting over several times and just couldn't do it. The yo-yo was broken. The days of losing weight only to gain it back were finished for me… and I was terrified. Whatever it was that had always reeled me back into the range of so called "normal weight" for much of my adult life was gone. Kaput. I was in trouble and not sure where to turn.

While on the weight rollercoaster, I had tried a lot of diets! My first one involved eating mostly meat and vegetables and taking mail-order diet pills. I joined a popular diet program on more than one occasion, only to fail miserably each time. On one occasion I ate so much broccoli that it took me years to face the stuff again. To this day I still have issues sometimes with spinach. The scariest thing was that I gained more weight after each diet. My high weight always continued to rise. I really believed that when I was uncomfortable enough, I could just diet and lose the weight I had gained. It had always worked for me before.

After my initial panic, I started to analyze why the diets and other programs I had been on had not brought me lasting weight-loss results. Even though I beat myself up for not having enough willpower, not exercising enough, and not being enough of whatever it was that made others model sized, I knew deep down that there was a physical/chemical component to this for me. Thanks to some wonderful alternate health care practitioners, I had learned over time that my body did not function well with sugar, flour, dairy, wheat, and some other common foods.

As I studied where things had gone wrong before, I came up with three things that I felt I needed to be successful: 1) I needed a food plan that completely eliminated sugar, flour and wheat; 2) I needed recipes to help me cook without these things, and 3) I needed a community of people who were supportive and who could help guide me through the process of losing the weight. As it turns out, that was my prayer to the Universe. I started to focus on those requirements and looked in my world to find evidence that they existed.

After a few months, I was guided to a 12-step program. It was at one of those meetings that I met Wendy. She was a huge support for me throughout the process. She told me about a food plan and another group that offered recipes as well as meetings. At first I was relieved and excited to know that what I had asked for really existed. Then I had to deal with my mind/body/spirit that was leery of going all out one more time for a little while, only to fail and return to an even higher weight.

I made my first commitment by choosing a date that I was going to start on the food plan. Then I sat down to the all-too-familiar task of creating a plan for the week so I could make my grocery list. I was paralyzed. I couldn't even put a plan on paper! I was stopped cold by the thought of more money spent on more food that was destined to rot in my refrigerator until the evidence of failure was thrown away in shame.

I finally convinced myself that I could plan one day's worth of meals and shop for one day's worth of food, and that's what I did. I started this new food plan literally focusing on getting through one day at a time. The next day, I planned the following day's meals and shopped for the following day's food. After the third day, I allowed myself to plan two days at a time, then three, and eventually, an entire week. The tiny steps – these babiest of baby steps - started me on the path. And what a path it was!

For over two years, I weighed and measured every bite that went into my mouth. I went to weekly meetings and communicated daily with others who were on my food plan. On top of this I married three months into the journey. I even weighed and measured all of my food at my wedding reception, and Wendy made food for me to take on my honeymoon! My sister was appalled when I pulled out my scale at a fine restaurant, but I did it anyway. I was committed to doing the plan with no slips and no relaxing of the rules, and that's what I did. Every day. Christmas, New Year's, my birthday - every single day. For the first time in my life I felt free. No cravings. No longings. No binges. It was remarkable.

During the course of the journey, I lost 106 pounds, and first made conscious contact with a power greater than myself. I realized that I had spent much of my life trying to control everything around me instead of focusing on what I could change about me to make myself happier. It wasn't always a smooth ride. I found that I had become adept at losing weight and at gaining it back, but I had no idea how to maintain my weight. The journey of maintenance has been an interesting one for me. The whole experience has been life changing, to say the least.

Usually I'm an evangelist for things that work for me when I think they might help others, but I have never suggested that people follow my food plan. Sometimes even I wasn't sure that it was worth it. Sure

I fit into smaller clothes, but I felt tired all of the time and I had some issues with my back in the early years of the weight loss. I knew that I needed to stay on the plan, regardless of what the immediate outcomes looked and felt like, and that's what I did.

As I took more ownership of my happiness, over time I found other resources that filled in some of the blanks, including a healing modality that turned into a spiritual practice for me. I have wonderful practitioners, colleagues, students, clients and family who have been an active part of my living my dream. The list of those who have helped me get where I am today continues to grow. I have realized that help is always there if we ask for it. It might not come from where we think it should come from, but it always comes if we pay attention.

I learned that each person has to take action for themselves and no one else. I couldn't lose weight for anyone else, and I could only focus on what I needed to put into my mouth without regard to anyone else. So my dear husband, who wasn't even my husband when I started the food plan, was left to fend for himself. It wasn't all a bed of roses and it's still not. Even now I still pay attention to what I eat and avoid foods that I know don't work well with my body.

I know that I'm still a work in progress, and that the progress I'm making in understanding myself and how Spirit and I work together is changing me and those around me. The absolute truth and love without judgment that I've come to know from that relationship makes it all worth it.

For you, the reader of my story, your challenge doesn't have to be about weight. You can change any part of your life or yourself that you feel is not in alignment with who you really are. First, know that you are worthy of having whatever you want, then determine what you want to work on. Next, find someone who can support you in making those changes. It can be a friend or even a coach that you hire. Know that there are people whose life purpose is to support people like you with issues like yours. When you own who you are, you become a changed person. When it's not about what others have done to you or what you have done to yourself, when you face where you are and move forward from there, your life begins to take a form that really, truly matches the real you. The wonderful, amazing, magnificent you that lies within.

Nancie Benson works with individuals and businesses to instantly change conscious and subconscious limiting beliefs and to empower them to design the future from their new perspective. She is a ThetaHealing™ practitioner and instructor, and a Reiki Master Teacher who uses energetic healing in spiritual mentoring and counseling, workshops, seminars, and keynote speeches. Write to Nancie@NancieBenson.com or access her Free report, Worthy to Achieve *at www.WorthyToAchieve.com.*

Second Chances

Kathleen Gage

Life was great. I had just landed my dream job working in the advertising department for a small radio station in Santa Rosa, California. Life couldn't be better. It hadn't always been this good.

It wasn't but a few years earlier that it had gotten so bad I ended up homeless and unemployable. At the time I was sure it was because I was simply destined to live a miserable life, hitting roadblock after roadblock.

I now know that this happened through the choices I had made, not by the hand I had been dealt. Actually, my childhood years had been pretty darned good.

Growing up, life was pretty average. I was raised by a loving father and mother, had two older sisters and the usual family pets: dogs, cats, hamsters, and a bird or two over the years.

My mother and father were good parents, loving all the time, yet stern when they had to be, and lenient when they could.

As a very young child I would often pick flowers for my mother and could more times than not be found by her side eager to help her in any way I could. We had a great relationship. Being the baby in the family gave me special privileges and I knew it, and felt very special because of it.

My dad was the best father I could hope for. Looking back I realize how blessed I was to have a dad who would take time to explain to a three year old why snow turns into water. Wiping the tears from my face while keeping a tight grip on the bucket I had carefully filled with the magical white flakes the night before that was now nothing more than a bucket of water, my dad gently explained how everything changes.

Always happy to be with my dad, I guess you could say I was daddy's little girl.

I don't remember when things began to change, but I do remember many a night when my parents would tell me how worried they were for my safety and plead with me to change my ways. I turned my gentle spirit to that of a harsh teenager who grew more distant and angry with each passing day.

I seemed to look for the roughest people I could find to hang out with and call my friends. It wasn't long before I was getting in trouble at virtually every turn and watching my life quickly spin out of control. What began as a fun way to live soon became a self made prison. And yet, like with any prison, I didn't know where to find the key to release me.

There were countless times I prayed to a nonexistent God asking for help. "I promise I will change my ways." For years the promises were empty pleas until one day I got a glimpse of where my life was and where it could be if I were willing to make much needed changes.

That glimpse allowed me to see things differently, a little at a time. First with a book, then a conversation, then a movie, then…. The answers had been there all along - I was just not able to see. Or maybe I just hadn't been willing, until not changing became more painful than changing.

In my early twenties I began a soul search and spiritual journey that allowed me to take responsibility for my life. I quit blaming others for my misfortunes, while slowly learning how to give to others, rather than always trying to get from others and become the person I was destined to be.

After nearly a decade of self-discovery I landed the job at the radio station. I remember being asked why they should hire me with so little sales experience. My response was simple: "Because I will give you the best of me I can. All I need is a chance."

My half hour commute to and from work gave me plenty of time to reflect on how far my life had come since those dark nights and empty days. Life was great and I didn't think anything could change it, until I received a call late one night about a month into my new job from my brother-in-law saying that if I wanted to see my father alive, I had better come quickly. He had suffered a major heart attack and was in a coma. The doctors didn't think he would make it through the night.

I thought of nothing but getting to my dad's bedside. In that moment much of what I had believed to be important became insignificant, including my new job.

I drove two hours in a fog of tears and regret. The tears were for the thought of never seeing my dad alive again, and the regret was for the many times I didn't take the opportunity to tell him the important things in life like, "I love you." As I drove through the night I vowed that if I were given another chance, I would never miss the opportunity again.

Most of the first night at my father's bedside is difficult to recall. I do remember calling my boss to tell her my father was in a deep coma and from one moment to the next we didn't know if he would make it. I went on to say that I didn't know when I would be in again. Until all was said and done, I hadn't realized how truly blessed I had been to get that job and that boss. She not only said don't worry about coming back until I was ready, she also told me I would continue to draw a paycheck, which was a huge relief.

When I walked into my father's room I was shocked at what I saw. Laying helpless and lifeless with tubes in every part of his body and on life support was the man who for so many years had prayed for me to find a better path in life. There lay the man who I was just beginning to have a relationship with after so many years of having pushed him away. This was a man who had been a loyal husband for over thirty-five years and a great example of someone who stood by his commitments.

After the first week of my dad's heart attack, it became apparent that my father might remain like this for quite some time, possibly never coming out of his deep sleep. Traveling to and from my father's bedside was made easier with the support I got from my boss, who soon became a trusted friend. I couldn't help but feel like her presence in my life was a huge miracle. I wondered how many people, if placed in the same situation, would have responded the same way as she did.

Over the following weeks there was so much healing that took place in my family. Old wounds were slowly mended between my mother, sisters, and myself.

Even though my father could not respond to my words of love to him, I sensed he could still feel my love.

When the weeks turned into nearly a month there was talk that my dad would likely stay this way indefinitely. I get God bumps when I think back to the first motion my dad made. First it was a slight movement of a finger. Soon the finger became two, then a hand, and then his eyes opened. Over the next few days he was waking from his sleep.

Sadly, his body was coming to life, but his words were confused and disoriented. He talked of bizarre things that had happened to him that we knew hadn't.

The greatest miracle was yet to come when little by little my dad became coherent. Wondering where he got the strange stories, we realized his experience was based on what had been on television for the twenty-eight days he'd been in a coma. The television had been turned on a lot during his stay. It was evident that what went into his subconscious became his reality.

What an amazing lesson to learn. To know that what we put in our heart, mind, and soul becomes our reality.

Over twenty-two years later, my life is amazing. My dad and I have a great relationship, as do my mom and I. Both are now in their eighties and married for over sixty years. I call them often, visit when I can, and never miss a chance to tell them how much I love them.

I wake up with gratitude on a daily basis because I was given a second chance to turn my life around. I realize I may not always be given another opportunity to change anything in my life and how important it is to be in resolve each and every day.

I feel truly blessed that with my mom and dad, I was given a second chance - one I am not willing to take for granted. I love you mom and dad. Always have, always will.

Kathleen Gage is an Internet marketing advisor, inspirational speaker, and bestselling author. She derives great pleasure in working with spiritually based speakers, authors, coaches, and entrepreneurs who are ready to share their message through books, online channels, and live presentations. Visit www.KathleenGage.com to sign up for her Free newsletter, Street Smarts Marketing & PR.

Listen to What Your Heart Already Knows

Lauren P. Salamone

One week after my appointment with my new neurologist, the phone rang.

"Lauren, can you come in right away? I think we've found the cause of your problem."

My *problem.*

Yes, that's definitely what the symptoms had become these past few months: one confusing *problem.*

Young and otherwise healthy, I had been slowly, inexplicably losing control over my muscles from the waist down. My doctor had ruled out MS, but couldn't explain what was causing my muscles to atrophy. She sent me to physical therapy, thinking perhaps I could work my way back to normal muscle control.

So, for three months I had endured grueling leg lifts and elastic band exercises in an attempt to revive my muscles. I exercised at home. I exercised at the PT office. I exercised at the gym. If I could have exercised in my sleep, I would have done so. With each visit, my physical therapist would measure my muscle coordination for signs of progress, only to report, "No improvement," and off I would go, determined to work harder, longer.

Now, finally, a neurologist had discovered the source of my problem!

I high-tailed it to his office, where I found him staring at my MRI shots illuminated on a screen in front of him. He pointed to a tumor the size of a robin's egg. "Myxopapillary ependymoma," he was saying, "…regenerative benign tumor located in a nerve sack in your lower spine. It won't be an easy surgery, but this has to come out as soon as possible."

I exhaled.

The good news: Finally, I knew the cause of my muscle disorder… and the tumor was benign.

The bad news: While my symptoms wouldn't get worse, I would not regain full use of my muscles. I just had to hope for some improvement.

Medical Treadmill

Two weeks later I was in full-day surgery, followed by morphine for six days, and then home for a painstaking three months of recuperation before I could even begin physical therapy for my back. Oh, and after that I would need to resume physical therapy for my muscles.

Needless to say, this wasn't the most comfortable period of my life.

Physically -- I dealt, one at a time, with the steps I needed to take to recover. However, mentally I found myself completely out of my comfort zone.

What Now?

Up until this point, I had always carefully planned what my next moves would be professionally. I would calculate each step with a clear outline of how to achieve it. Then I would move forward feeling safe and grounded, ready to work hard in my next position. That was my pattern - that was my comfort zone.

But here I was with no idea of what I would physically be capable of doing. I expected to need more flexibility in my schedule than I was used to, but I didn't really know what my needs would be yet. How could I plan my next steps?

My most recent career had been as a high school English teacher. Clearly, running from class to class and living by the bell schedule wasn't going to work for me. I had planned to move on to a position as an executive trainer, but hadn't had the opportunity to fully take on my new responsibilities because of my medical condition. Would I be able to work full-time at that job at some point in the future?

It was scary, but in this forced place of discomfort I had no choice but to mentally exhale for the first time in my working life. There was no outline I could follow, nor place of safety from which I could plan. So, instead I reflected. I meditated. I began to do something I never would have otherwise done: *I allowed myself to dream.* And as a seed emerged, I actually gave myself permission to cultivate it.

I started to think about how many gratifying interactions I had enjoyed as a result of my years as a high school English teacher. Specifically, I focused on the many students who had sought my advice when they made that challenging transition from high school to college. Time and time again I had guided students over the same types of hurdles while they were in college, and a pattern of issues had emerged. I realized I had an arsenal of information to share. Thus began an acknowledgement of my calling to help as many students as I could to be confident and successful as they navigated their college years. I had no idea how I would make this dream a reality, but I was excited that I had allowed a true passion that was uniquely mine to surface! So, for the first time in my life, I began a journey towards a dream rather than a clearly attainable goal. I decided to trust that the answers to how I would do it would also surface… if I just paid attention.

Enter – The Doubt

I thought I would like to write a book, for one thing. Naturally, a voice in my head immediately retorted, "Who do you think you are? Write a book? Help students succeed in college? There isn't even a name for the career you are considering here!"

So I followed the strategies I had shared with my students over the years:

- **Take a Leap of Faith** – Once you've set your intention, move forward in faith, keeping your goal firmly in sight.

- **Ignore Doubt** – Learn to laugh at doubt to keep it from sabotaging your dream.

- **Look for Opportunities** – Begin to act upon the opportunities and signs that arise as you carry out Steps 1 and 2.

It Really Does Work!

That was two years ago. I've really had to stay focused on my commitment to follow the steps, but the signs and opportunities have come as a result. Here are two examples:

One day I couldn't seem to shake my doubt over whether I would ever be able to write my book or find a publisher for it, and I was on the brink of giving up. While in the grip of this frustration, I pushed – and really had to force myself – to shift my energy, to move away from this daunting vibe. I decided to clean and organize with the goal of lightening my work space.

In so doing, I came across a note from my father:

"Dear Lauren,
The first book is the hardest.
Love, Dad"

Inspiring for sure, but more than you might imagine because my dad passed away nearly 20 years ago. That was long before I ever dreamed of writing a book!

Why had he written these words? I'm not sure, but suffice it to say I headed right back to the computer... after a good cry.

On another occasion, I learned of a conference that was exactly on target with much of what I teach and believe. In order to keep harmony in my marriage, I had agreed not to spend money I didn't have on my business idea. So, to send out my intention in the meantime, I took what money I did have – a bold step for me – and signed up for a less expensive opportunity offered by the same teacher.

Within three days of making this decision, I received an e-mail with an apology and an unprecedented offer. The teacher had to cancel the less expensive workshop so was inviting me to the big conference instead. I was incredibly blessed to attend this life-changing conference one month later for one-tenth the cost paid by the other participants.

I could go on and on with these stories, but in each case the sign or opportunity came as the result of my conscious effort to move forward in faith.

Dreams Come True

It has been an amazing journey. Stepping out from this place of belief has resulted in success for me – and for so many college students – with much more to come. The feedback I receive from students, parents, and deans is abundantly gratifying. I am a guest speaker, a mentor and a coach. I belong to mastermind groups that help keep me inspired and in top form. And I am living well with my muscle disorder, which is pretty much undetectable to those around me at this point. To top it off, I came home one day to a message from an editor who wanted to know whether my book was still available to be published! (It's coming out in 2010!) Had I not experienced my challenging medical year, I never would have allowed myself to realize my dream. Misfortune can actually lead us to a place of joy we wouldn't otherwise know. Whatever challenge you face, I hope you will allow yourself to recognize a meaningful opportunity that may arise as a result. Play soothing music, light a candle, mentally exhale, and listen to your heart. You will be delighted by what you hear.

Lauren P. Salamone inspires college students with her philosophy that a positive transformation in college brings with it the power to enjoy a dynamic and abundant life. Her book, How To Be U, *hits bookstores in late Spring 2010. To receive a complimentary subscription to her motivational e-zine,* Time-Tested Tips to Help You Love College! *visit www.CollegeGuidanceGuru.com.*

When All Else Fails, There is Magic

Steven V. Rotz

I hung up the phone dejected. Another rejection! For the fourth time a deal for the 27,000 square foot alley building had fallen apart. For the same reason every time, the building needed too much. It would take me three to six months to find a buyer and three to six months to close a deal. If I could close it. The seller wasn't going to be happy and I was ready to move on.

The deal that had just fallen apart was with an investor. We were going to form a partnership. He would put up the money and I would manage the redevelopment. He liked the way I worked and wanted to do a project with me. He did not like the prospect of cleaning this property up and having industrial space in an alley. This property was going to require a lot of work for any tenant to want to be there.

I had a meeting with an advisor and was lamenting my poor fortune. He said I ought to buy it myself. While I had wanted to buy the property, I had not considered buying it solely on my own.

After twenty-four years in the commercial real estate business, it was time to work for myself. I decided to work through the process to see if I could make this building work for me. The challenging part would be finding a tenant that could see the potential in this out of date industrial building, and finding a bank willing to give me all the money to do the renovations and cover closing costs. I had some assets, but I had no significant capital available to invest in this project. Really, the only thing I had to start with was my expertise in commercial building real estate sales. I had in-depth knowledge in this area and had made many people money through this venue.

I'd been selling and leasing commercial buildings for about twenty-four years at that time, and I knew what the banks looked for when financing these properties. I knew what the zoning laws would permit and I had been working for a client that needed a location for a drug and rehabilitation center. The County Mental Health Department wanted a treatment center and had hired a vendor to provide these services and find a location. This property was ideal for that use, plus the vendor was very excited about this site. The neighborhood was sort of industrial and there would only be a few apartment buildings beside the facility.

The deal wasn't moving, so I went to a commissioners meeting and the Director for the Mental Health department put me on the agenda where I informed them what could be done to this property. They were very polite and let me give my pitch. Thirty days later the Director said they wanted a different site. Back to square one again. The Director knew and liked the building and location, as he had played on the second floor when his Dad worked there! He was working on a new set of services for people with mental illness. These services would help prevent people from needing intensive care at a hospital or mental health institution. He wanted to provide a community-based set of services to support getting people back on their feet. By now the Director had hired a vendor to provide these services and had asked this company to tour the building. The Director of Operations for the vendor did so and loved it.

While I was working with the County, I was also looking for additional funding. I had control of the building, but I was going to need to borrow the purchase price, closing costs, and enough money to make the building presentable to a potential tenant.

I went to the bank I had been dealing with for my commercial brokerage business and showed them how I could buy the building for half the appraised value. (I had an appraisal from one of the previous failed deals.) The owner now understood the building needed a complete renovation. I still had two tenants using 8,000 square feet of the 27,000, so I had enough rent to cover an interest only loan of $300,000. The bank approved $200,000 for the purchase and $100,000 for closing costs and cleaning the building up to make it look presentable as a shell.

The vendor for these new mental health services saw the potential. I had the property freshly painted, the old lights re-hung with new bulbs, and the old offices demolished. It was a shell ready to begin redeveloping. Thankfully this time the County Commissioners liked it as well.

I took the plunge and bought the building. Within six months I was able to relocate the main tenant, and the mental health services company leased 90% of the building's square footage.

The county wanted to help defray the rent expense, so they gave the vendor $1,700,000 towards the complete renovation costs. The vendor in turn made that money available to me to start some of the necessary work, as well as paying a fair rent for a commercial building shell.

Today the property houses a twenty-six bed state of the art mental health center, complete with a greenhouse, fountain, ceramics program area, sanctuary and group area for the wellness program, and gardens. The facility is the first non-hospital-based Acute Care Mental Health Services facility in the country. It changed the facility's concept from institution to home, through collaboration with the state, county, vendor, and myself, the developer.

The new appraised value came in at $3.45 million dollars.

The equity created in this property allowed my wife and me to purchase a 20,000 square foot building for her wellness center, Agape Healing Center. The mental health company used many of the wellness concepts from Agape in developing their treatment programs.

I was able to create about $1,500,000 of equity by overcoming my initial fears of going into business for myself. I did more for building my net worth in one transaction than I had working for twenty-three years for someone else. I was instrumental in developing a new type of facility and the services offered there. The company hired my wife's business, Agape Healing Center, to provide two days of training to the staff of the facility. I was able to get financing for 150% of the purchase price. I was also able to get three times the industrial rent on the building by getting it rezoned from industrial to a commercial services facility. Additionally, I was able to get a mental health facility approved in a residential neighborhood at the local Zoning Board, and in return I obtained an infinite return on capital.

I found that I love working on old buildings and that I was more than competent at re-developing them to be very attractive, functional, and to provide a superior environment for the tenants, all the while making money and providing rents below market norms.

What surprised me the most was the way everything came together to create a project that can only be described as magical. The whole far exceeded the sum of each of the parts. I created wealth and income, and when the project was finished it was worth more than the total dollars invested into it. When I calculated my profits I had attained an infinite return.

I learned that I had developed all the skills necessary to create a fantastic real estate investment, but I think the most important lesson learned was that I needed to commit to working through the process to see if I could make this property work.

That sounds simple, but the biggest obstacle most of us budding entrepreneurs face is the difficulty we have in committing to making something work. Once I committed to trying to make this property work, I discovered how action, knowledge, and passion can combine to create magical results.

Steve Rotz is the principal owner of Rotz Commercial Realty in Pennsylvania. He has been in the field of real estate sales for twenty-eight years and is a member of the Society of Industrial and Office Realtors® (SIOR). He has successfully redeveloped a 200,000+ square feet old industrial type building. Visit www.Rotz.net to download your Free copy of How to Find Money to Start Investing in Real Estate.

When Grace Comes to Get You

Barbara McCollough

When I was invited to participate in a book project called Overcomers Inc., I jumped at the chance. I thought it would be fun to work with others on a writing project, and I knew I would learn a ton. The only problem, I thought, was that I couldn't think of a single thing that I had overcome.

I thought about this for days and days. I began to think that I was one of those rare people who had such a wonderful life that I was never fully tested, that circumstances never called forth from me any such heroism that I could lay claim to.

Overcoming? Surely I had overcome something. Everything I thought of was so bland, I decided I had to withdraw from the project.

The next morning I awoke remembering a time I hadn't thought of for many years. I was twenty four years old, a college grad, newly separated from a marriage whose ink had barely dried on the certificate, living again in my parents' house, and commuting every day into Washington D.C. to work at my government job in the area of classification and pay management. Boring! I remember the gray Selectric typewriter, the gray metal desk, the gray walls… *ZZZZ*. I was beyond miserable. I was a corpse propped up at a desk.

Then one day, sitting at my desk, something inside me just woke up. Like a ball of energy in the middle of my belly, it propelled me to the typewriter where "it" typed the following in one go:

I'm on my way,
I don't know where,
Don't know where my day is bound
To take me.
To heights I've never been nor known,
To places I can feel, not see.
I know your bags are packed to go,
So why not take the trip with me?

Affirmation's all we need,
A thought, a look…the silent deed,
To know reality un-obscured,
By all that's gone before.

If love consists in truly giving,
What finer gifts might we bestow,
Than the wonder of thought from our timeless minds,
Untaintable, impregnable and whole.

When "it" was done I sat back in amazement. I had never written a poem, if that's what this was. Who was the I? Who was the you? Three days later I quit my job and embarked on a cross-country journey, knowing only that the "trip" that was announced to me was not to be found in the daily scoot of my rolling chair beneath the gray metal desk. It would take me to places I could feel, not see.

I wondered, "Could this memory have something to do with the Overcomers book? If so, what?" I finally got it.

This incident totally changed my relationship to "overcoming" - to relying upon my will alone to make major changes in my life. I had always believed that any success in my life would be achieved through hard work and the occasional lucky break of being in the right place at the right time. Yet at the age of twenty four, try as I might, I was seemingly unable to figure out how to move my life in a direction I wanted it to go. I might have been in the right time, but I surely wasn't in the right place.

How can I explain this moment when inspiration broke through in the form of the poem and led me from paralysis into action?

I can't. Or not in ways the linear mind can report. A teacher once told me that the path to a fulfilling life was like the flight of a two winged bird: one wing was self-effort and the other grace. Without both, a bird won't fly and neither will our lives. Dogged adherence to effort can take you right into a place you don't even want to go, yet simply waiting for inspiration without accompanying action leads to paralysis (insightful paralysis perhaps, but still paralysis). It is the true partnership of self-effort and grace—inspired action – that is the secret to success.

If I were to frame my experience as overcoming an obstacle, perhaps what I overcame was a tendency to let my ego do the driving. I opened myself to that mysterious other force that we all know and describe in our own unique way, that we can never control, but we can always depend upon.

A spiritual teacher of mine, many years after the typewriting incident, defined ego to me like this: "The ego is a twig, floating on the current of a stream, believing it is charting its course."

I liked that. I began to see that underlying current as the source of inspired action. I started to pay attention to ways it showed itself in my life, trusting its urgings more than any plan I had made.

The path that took me out of the government job meandered here and there for a time, and one year later I found myself, against all odds, applying to a single, hard to get into graduate school in social work. When I was accepted, I went with fifty dollars in my pocket and no idea where the rest of the money would come from, but it did. The stream, it seems, had a pretty hefty current.

As I prepared to go, I remembered a little book that I had found and read during my stint at the gray metal desk - a book describing the oldest hospital-based social work department in the country, namely Massachusetts General Hospital. Three months after I began graduate school, we were all assigned our clinical internships across the country. I smiled when I saw that I had been assigned to Mass. General.

I have come to understand how our lives have their own shape and destiny. Even if it is destiny, I believe we have free choice, and that choice is whether we go where our lives are trying to lead us willingly and happily, or fight it all the way. If I was meant to be in Boston, even if I hadn't heeded the poem so long ago, I trust that I would have come via another route, but perhaps one on which I would have had to overcome many obstacles. Perhaps I would have had to overcome the fact that I had no money to go to graduate school. Perhaps I would have had to put a lot of energy into figuring out my career path, or I would have had to overcome the rigors of applying to multiple schools to increase my odds at getting a spot in at least one school. Perhaps in the end it would have been the exact same outcome, but a very different journey.

As I write this, I have just two days ago closed my thirty year long private practice in psychotherapy. Why? I have developed a more sophisticated way of explaining causes for my behavior, but essentially it was for the same reason I left my government job in classification and pay management. Six months ago, an inner voice instructed me to do this. That same calm, yet strong inner voice said it was time. It was not at all affected by the countervailing voice that wanted to argue about income, savings and retirement funds and disappointing others. When it says done, I am done.

We all have this connection to the guidance from within, regardless of what we call it or our varying ability or willingness to heed it. Think back on your life when you followed a hunch (or even when you didn't and in the end wished you had). These can be the simplest of moments upon which the trajectory of your life turns. Chances are that any time you look back at important turning points and think, "It all began when…" you are actually remembering a moment when your inner wisdom led you to make a life altering choice.

The most important ingredient is your own willingness to pay attention, to not dismiss urgings to go in directions that feel right, but don't make logical sense. Your inner wisdom knows where your heart yearns to go, often long before your conscious mind does, and it also knows how to get you there.

It is discerning the promptings that's the hard part. It is getting your mind, that ego we were talking about, out of the way so it won't talk you out of following your heart. One of the easiest ways to do this is to be around others who will understand and support you, who will urge you toward your own inspired action.

On your path to fulfillment, you don't have to row upstream, and you don't have to get in the boat alone.

*To find out the surprising place **Barbara McCollough's** inner voice led her after closing her psychotherapy practice, go to www.barbaramccollough.com. While you are there, be sure to download her free report* Say Yes Quickly: The Key to Inspired Action.

My Crazy, Beautiful Life Makeover

Karen L. Keeney

Life is filled with new beginnings. We start school, new jobs, get married, and some of us have kids. Most of those events are joyful beginnings. However, I remember the first day of junior high as one of the worst days of my life. I couldn't find my math class, walked in late, and everyone turned and stared at me. Plus the teacher was mean, and of course, I had cramps.

So, here I am now at fifty; another new beginning. I needed to make some big changes in my life. I was stressed out, unhappy and not so healthy. Only this time, I am not really lost, I just don't know exactly where I am going. The only eyes on me are my husband's and the dog's, and yet again, I have cramps. (More about the dogs and the cramps later; they are part of my makeover.) I start this year forging ahead to the next fifty years of my life. (This is the first time I have written about that number; I am not sure how I feel about it.) It is time for some big changes.

It is December 18, 2008. I was laid off on the same day my husband had back surgery. Losing my job is not unfamiliar territory for me. In fact, the family discussion each year is how many W2's Karen will have. Although being unemployed is nothing new, it was unexpected and not great timing. My husband will be off work recovering for a while and we have never been out of work at the same time. I try to picture the two of us together seven days a week, twenty four hours a day until I find another job. Twenty-eight years of marriage, two grown kids still at home, I am not sure how this will go. What am I going to do? I make the decision not to get another job, but to start my own company and work from home. Thus commences part one of my crazy, beautiful life makeover. Some people would say it takes a lot of courage to start your own business in 2009 when the economy is unstable. I'm not sure about that. Courage was my son's decision when on September 12, 2001 at the age of seventeen, he and several of his friends would enlist in the military to defend our country. Courage was him climbing on a plane on September 11, 2002 heading to Iraq. My decision to not get a "real job" is not really all that brave.

During part two of my makeover I got a puppy! My little, black and white cutest-puppy-in-the-world named CJ. I can't tell you how hard I fell for this little guy. We are attached at the hip. He follows me from room to room, sleeps in our bedroom at night. We play, walk, and cuddle. I can tell you there is nothing better than getting kisses filled with puppy breath to take away any stress. I truly believe that he is one of the factors that helped my blood pressure go down! There is evidence that proves that having a pet is good for your health and I believe it. In the first couple of weeks with CJ I wondered about this crazy decision, especially while out in the dark of my backyard in my nightgown in the middle of the night so he can go potty. I can't tell you how nervous I was the first time I left him home alone with my husband. We worked through it all and now CJ is my special little boyfriend. I needed more love in my life and he does it for me!

Which brings me back to the cramps and part three of my make-over - hormones!

All I can say is that I didn't think the impending big "change" would be like this. Waking up from a dead sleep with my pulse racing and sweat dripping from places I didn't know even had sweat glands; what is that about? My doctor explained it to me saying, "Your hormones are like a house full of teenagers with no adults home." That says it all. She suggested that women my age respond really well to yoga and meditation because it helps this biological stage of my life. Now I spend time in my family room posing like a pigeon, a monkey, a swan, or a dog, but I actually do feel better. I also started jogging. This is one of the crazy parts because if anyone knew how much I hate jogging (I definitely mean hate!) they would never believe that I willing choose to do it. My two secret weapons? My Ipod™ and good shoes! If I play the music loud enough, I can't hear my gasps for air or hear my feet pounding on the sidewalk. I just run through several songs until I make it back home. I sometimes listen to inspirational speakers who teach about the laws of the universe as related to wealth, which has given me a new perspective about money. I love to hear about abundance. I want to learn about the laws that make me sure I am stepping into my true purpose in life. I still wouldn't say I really enjoy jogging, but at least my feet don't hurt, and I did figure out what runner's high is all about. When I commit to jogging on Mondays, Wednesdays and Fridays, I get my runner's high on Tuesdays and Thursdays!

I don't eat wheat anymore, which may sound crazy. I don't eat bread, pasta, and I don't eat cookies. (Well, not exactly no cookies at all. I have one or two instead of the whole package.) I found out I have wheat intolerance. I read somewhere that some women found their brain worked better and the fog lifted when they gave up wheat. If I could remember where I read that I would share it, but my fog hasn't completely lifted yet.

There is also an actual makeover in this story. I redecorated my office to create a beautiful environment that inspires me as I coach my clients, write, read and listen to uplifting music, audio meditations and programs by successful mentors. Beside my desk I have a beautiful painting of a beach in Portugal where my husband's family emigrated from; a beach on which we will sit one day. I have a great vision board that is filled with pictures and written aspirations which keep me focused on the things I want to attract into my life. I chose tropical-style furniture and accessories that remind me how much I love to travel. The star of my office decor is my desk which is my grandmother's sewing machine cabinet (with her sewing machine still in it), which she gave me before she died. It reminds me of her: a woman who worked back when it wasn't popular for women to have jobs. She created beauty every time she sat at her machine and made clothes. She taught me how to sew, taught me about my roots, and she taught me to speak my mind. (You never had to wonder what she was thinking!)

My crazy, beautiful life makeover is in full swing now and I've moved into a wonderful time of my life! My days are filled with writing, creating, and dreaming. I have the privilege of coaching clients, hearing victory in their voices. I work in an office I love to spend time in, surrounded by my memories of my grandma, along with my visions of the future. I love snuggling with CJ. I spend time just breathing. I have faith that I am here to do this work. I spend time reading and listening to inspirational teachings by successful people. I am learning about the Laws of the Universe and about how much God wants us all to live in abundance. I am becoming the best role model for other women by living my life's purpose so I can inspire them to do the same. For my husband and me, this has been a time of reconnecting. I know when the kids have left our house we won't be sad or lonely, as we will be friends who enjoy each other's company. (I get the feeling he is getting ready for his own crazy, beautiful life makeover.)

I am so glad I've taken the time to create an environment of love and beauty and to do things that make me healthier. I look for beauty in all I do and spend time learning to trust God. How lucky I am to have been laid off! How lucky I am to have attracted all of this beauty into my life. I pray my next fifty years will continue even crazier and more beautiful! I can't wait to see what comes next!

Since 1989, **Karen Keeney** *has been coaching and helping independent business women to reach their potential and make more money. For the last several years Karen has worked as corporate Trainer for several companies, ranging from small start-up companies to large established corporations. She knows first-hand what works and what does not work in running a successful business. Visit her at www.KarenLKeeney.com and register for her newsletter,* Success With Purpose.

Finding My Purpose Through Adversity and Practical Experience

Nachhi Randhawa

In the spring of 2005, my family and I were shaken by one of the most tragic events of our lives when my husband, an only child, lost his father suddenly one morning from a heart attack. Through many dark days of despair and sleepless nights, we fought our way to re-connect within ourselves and with life, to reface the world as we now knew it to be. And through the grief-ridden days, the world still kept moving and so did our real-world jobs.

As we continued working each day, I started facing some serious disconnects from my years spent in the corporate world. The fire that was once there, which helped me land some of the most prestigious positions right out of college, was starting to dwindle. The years had worn on my young age - the contentment was no longer there. I would go to work each day, put in the best I could, then go home - and wonder what true fulfillment was. What was life really? What is our greater purpose? Is this all there is to life? What about all the creative energy within? What could one do there and how could one unleash that?

One difficult family tragedy had me questioning life like I had never done. Was it enough to just work, come home, cook, and spend a little time with my family? Inside I yearned for something I had hidden for years. In high school and college, my first love was always speaking and writing. Yet I considered that a "hobby" and never thought it was something I could get paid to do. So, I studied for a "real degree" that would get me a "real job." Certainly it did, as upon receiving my degree I was offered a management position for a Fortune 500 company where I earned some wonderful opportunities as I climbed the management ladder.

Then along came marriage and shortly after, a relocation to a similar management position. As the perks and rewards came, so did the responsibilities. I worked and enjoyed the rewards, happy that I was thriving in the workplace. In 2001, our beautiful daughter came into the world and stole our hearts and our waking hours. This little precious gem from God deserved so much more than a mommy that worked eleven to twelve hours a day and then some with being on-call. So, we purchased our first home and I made the biggest decision of my life at that time, namely to stay home and raise my precious little angel. After a couple years at home, I started missing the work force again. Looking back I think it was a balance I was seeking, so back to the corporate world I went.

Now in late 2005, I sat at a crossroads wondering about the next step that my life would take. Where did I go from here? What was my purpose? How could I create a fulfilling day every single moment, day in and day out? The more questions I asked, the more I started to experience some serious inner shifts. I started reading and going through the dozens of books I had on my shelf. I was especially fond of the works of Dr. Wayne W. Dyer, ever since I'd seen him on a television special in early 2001. Dr. Dyer was my first spiritual teacher and I continue to live by much of what I have learned from his teachings. I went on to explore other works from similar thought leaders, and was astounded by learning and tying in our mind-reality connections. I was fascinated and knew I was onto something.

As I toyed with my thoughts and my new found knowledge of our inner thoughts creating our outer realities, my insights and intuitive nudges started to prove themselves time and again. My first big encounter with this came in June 2006, when my husband was offered a position which would take us three hours closer to our families. We had to quickly think of selling our home, and with a little research we decided to sell it ourselves. Being the logical people that we are, every step had to be calculated very carefully, as the economy was increasingly sluggish and some houses had been on the market for months.

Life sure surprised me on that fateful day in June as I drove home and upon turning the corner of our street, I had the most profound feeling that our house had to go on the market that very moment. I rushed home and shared this urgency with my family. Suddenly, propelled by a force stronger than me, within minutes I had created a quick flyer and hung a "For Sale" sign in our front yard. The very next day a young couple called and came to see the house. Instantly I had a connection and knew this couple were the new owners. Two days later we drew up the sales contract.

We moved to the new town and I continued learning more about our mind-body connections and the depth of our human potential. Again, I continued to witness how my faith in the universal powers would literally bring me what I was creating in my mind. One fine example was when I was distraught with my long commute to work and lacking fulfillment in my current job. I sat on the side of my bed somewhere between despair and hope, asking and writing a "Dear God" note to find me the perfect position with the perfect benefits and flexibility for my family life. The next day I knew exactly where to apply. Soon after I was called for an interview and was immediately offered the position.

Life was teaching me a lot about the inner workings of our mind and how faith in life could literally create anything and everything as we vision it in our minds. Once again this was proven when we found our dream house within two days of setting a clear intention, back in November 2007. As I sat on the concrete-stamped patio bench, I knew I was home.

Now I knew enough to know that my purpose was not in the corporate world. While I had figured that out perhaps a few years before, I guess I had to really experience these changes to know that I had a gift that I needed to share and support others in living their dream life. So, in November 2008, my business was born. I did my first official workshop in December and had an amazing turnout. In January 2009, I started building my online networking groups and met the most incredible people. Within two months, I had an inspirational video creation and was a featured guest on an online radio show.

At last through all the hard work and searching a very deep part within me, simply by asking some very real truths of my greater purpose in life, it seems that the glue was starting to bond me to this purpose. Every single day I see evidence all around me of the important work that I am here on this earth for, and the very reasons that I must carry it out. Starting this business has totally brought a world of movers and shakers into my life, joining in a global revolution of unity and service. We are all students and teachers to each other.

One of the biggest things I have learned in business is that by giving true value, others flock instantly to you, and the universe conspires to line up the perfect opportunities at the perfect timing. With that faith held in the highest of regards within ourselves, those opportunities usually appear magically at the most opportune and divine timings. As you take hold of these opportunities, you literally step into another world, a world outside of worlds where there are no fears, and your light starts to shine in every corner of all those whom you come into contact with.

The many teachers and mentors I have learned from over the years have been the fountains of my wealth and insights. That said, my biggest tip for starting on this path would be to put your own self-education first. Simply start with asking yourself all the questions you have hidden inside, then journaling your reflections to those questions, and daily inspirational reading for at least 30 minutes. There is an incredible wealth of knowledge right at your fingertips if you allow yourself to open up to it. Through your own search and curiosity, you will be moved to sharing your most personal talents and gifts as spirit would have you. I've personally seen this from doing things blindly, to living simply by sight, and now living completely by faith, how life can totally take you to levels unimagined. This work is so much more than healing your life and finding your purpose. It's about truly living life and reclaiming yourself!

Nachhi Randhawa is a speaker, Heal Your Life® Teacher, prosperity and life purpose facilitator, and owner of Grand Life Solutions. Nachhi inspires and supports individuals in living a spiritually conscious life while empowering them to tap into their own healing, awakening, and living their grand purpose. Visit Nachhi and get her Free Meditation, Relax and Achieve Your Dreams *as well as her* Grand Life Success Kit, *at www.GrandLifeSolutions.com.*

The Weed That Broke Through the Sidewalk

Marifran Korb

On our twenty-third wedding anniversary, it was dramatically clear that my life would never be the same. Emotionally unrestrained, my husband pushed me physically for the first time. It signaled he was out of control.

For all the years we were married, he had pushed me away emotionally, yet he was not a monster. Mostly, his love was strong and his humor was swift. He had no dreadful habits, only terrible moods. Anger made our marriage hard to reconcile, and love made it hard to leave. I'd habituated to his dark, irritable ways.

This time, something snapped in me. Approaching midlife, I realized his inexplicable behavior would never disappear. I saw my future flash before me. Predictably, it looked remarkably like my past.

While the timing was terrible, I resolved to take control. Having quit my job of twelve years the day before, I still could not allow the lack of income to stop me. Deciding to leave a job when I felt disrespected gave me the resolve to leave my relationship that disempowered me.

So, how did I get to this place? Slowly. Gradually I suspected, and then realized, my husband was seriously depressed. Right after our marriage started, he exploded over small upsets. Little things like a window smudge, a wrinkled bedspread, or a traffic jam. Any reason was enough for blowups that were sudden, loud, and frequent. Starting quickly, they passed rapidly like a summer rain. While I ignored the explosions, I tensely waited for the next wave to surface.

Increasingly, I had reason to worry. When our daughter was born, Ed's flare-ups increased in number and severity. Minor irritations became major. He was a walking volcano, ready to burst with the hot lava of fury.

Ed wouldn't reveal what really was wrong. He didn't know. When asked during the day, he would say he was too busy to talk. At night, he'd say he was too tired. At times, he told me that he just wanted to go to sleep and never wake up.

By his thirties, Ed's skin took on a gray pallor. Besides having no patience, he had the look of the walking dead. His work hours got oppressively long. Even through his cancer treatments, the escalating explosions expanded.

Observing that some members of his family had similar anger symptoms, I gently began suggesting that he had inherited depression. Surprisingly, he agreed wholeheartedly.

Next, I repeatedly requested that Ed get help to treat his depression. It wasn't his fault. He didn't mean to be that way, but he was, and only he could turn it around. He responded with procrastination, excuses, and inaction.

Meanwhile, Ed often had close encounters with job loss due to temper outbursts that were mild compared to what happened at home. Yet, I'd tell myself it wasn't so bad. Secretly I hid my pain from others, since I knew his devoted side. "I must be wrong for being dissatisfied," I figured.

Sometimes I told Ed how his emotional distance and his upsets affected me. Sharing my perspective never went well, and I always felt worse for it.

That "pushed" day, I told Ed I was prepared to leave "Depression Valley," with him or without him. My ultimatum was that I'd stay if he sought professional help. Reaching deep for self-love, I recognized that I also was loving him by refusing to stay in an unhealthy situation. By allowing his behavior, I was supporting his disease, delaying his progress, and injuring my soul. His depression went untreated, while I was busy enduring. Fearing that medicine would erase his identity, Ed was not ready to choose medication.

Though my strength had been a sense of responsibility, making the marriage work no matter what, I had not required Ed's responsibility for the marriage. Also, I was not being responsible for my happiness. On that day, I stood up for the possibility of living every day with joy, rather than surviving another day as I had.

While I knew that my husband could not control his dark moods, I was unwilling to give up on him. Yet, I had given up on me, as if I didn't matter.

Ed's unprovoked anger was forever smoldering, waiting to erupt. While feeling unappreciated and stressed for years, I finally confronted the truth that I was unable to save him from himself. I had to risk it all to reclaim myself.

We parted as a couple and continued as friends. Recognizing his behavior and realizing how it had affected me, he described my strength as, "The weed that broke through the sidewalk," suggesting he was the sidewalk.

Before I moved out, many friends spread the word that I was separating, while remaining friends with Ed. Many wanted to know how I did that, and they shared with me their marital pain. That was how I began coaching people about relationships. People insisted on paying me for what I could tell them about re-structuring an old relationship with love. My business, Soulful Solutions, was born then, and continues today seventeen years later. Thankfully, the universe supported me with business, and other miracles.

My choice for happiness for myself proved the right change for Ed, too. When he looked at himself and his life, he decided two years later that he could no longer tolerate depression. Facing deep fears, he took an anti-depressant, and discovered he could be both happy and himself. Within two weeks he was a changed man. Everyone noticed a marked difference.

Three years after becoming a peaceful, contented man, he entertained the idea of us living together. Having lived apart for five years and doing fine, we both wondered if we truly could successfully live together. After discussing it for hours, we were surprised that what we each wanted to give was just what we both wanted to receive.

Starting over has resulted in both of us being happier beyond our wildest dreams. We found the delight and self-expression we wanted. Once apart for five years, now we have been back together for twelve delightful, fun-filled, precious years. As a Joint Adoration Society, our motto is:

Together we evolve, joyful, healthy, triumphant partners
in the dance of life!

Here are some things I learned through my journey:

- Staying in an unsatisfactory marriage kills your spirit and your spouse's, no matter who is the primary cause.

- You cannot take responsibility for a spouse who refuses to address his health issues. (Chronic depression is a **physical** problem manifesting emotionally).

- The universe is always supporting you, even though you often resist the next step.

- You own your life, and must take responsibility for your happiness and satisfaction.

- Despite the fact that you have not lived on your own for decades, as a single person again you can find your talents, support yourself financially, and experience full satisfaction.

- Friends are everywhere. Many old friends and new people show up.

- Separating can result in blessings you never imagined.

- Eventually, you may support others who have similar experiences.

Every marital situation is different. My story is not a prescription for other unhappy marriages to follow. It is an example of what may be a possible solution in some situations. What I recommend is applying courage whenever needed. **At every juncture in your life, tune into your courage by listening to your inner guidance.**

Marifran Korb is a Relationship Rejuvenator Coach, living with her husband in Cincinnati, Ohio. Volunteering for The Hunger Project, she desires the end of both physical and emotional hunger. Traveling internationally and dancing locally are also her passions. For more information on coaching, visit www.SoulfulSolutions.com. To receive a free Relationship Styles Booklet, go to www.SoulfulSolutions.net.

Decide to Go Seek: Overcoming Life's Chronic Little Challenges to Let Your Purpose Shine Through

Julio Blanco

It took me a while to put the pieces of life's puzzle together. And by a while I mean the better part of two decades. I had long sensed a purpose awaiting me beyond my corporate career, and the desire to live this purpose intensified with time, but boy, was I slow. It took years at a turtle's pace to discover my life's true purpose and act on it.

I had to overcome serious obstacles to get here, the biggest one being... me. Along the way I learned that life's challenges come in two varieties. Sometimes we face acute challenges such as a life-threatening illness or accident, the death of a loved one, a job loss, or a business failure. Trials like these knock you right down and force you to deal with life on very stark terms. Live or die. Eat or starve. Thrive or fail.

The more common experience, however, involves the murkier, chronic challenges that bless and plague all of us. While often slow and subtle, they are no less significant. They come in a jumble of forms that mix and mesh in tangled webs. They include your fears and unhealed emotional wounds. They lurk in countless limiting beliefs about your potential. They often manifest in self-defeating behaviors and addictions that compensate for perceived lost love and security, or self-esteem we crave to regain. Most of all, they are rooted in our ignorance about the presence of a loving Spirit that longs to see you live the equally loving purpose for which you were created. And it's all yours to have if you will just decide to receive it.

My own life is a lesson in challenges of the chronic kind. Plagued by self-doubt and low self-confidence much of my adult life, I still enjoyed a pretty successful 18 year corporate career by most standards. For the majority of it I was a consumer marketer in Fortune 500 companies. The first decade went quite well as I enjoyed the work and the people, was quite good at it, and was promoted several times. The positive feedback received during that time also boosted the self-confidence I'd largely lost during a rather lonely adolescence.

Despite this positive trajectory, it was obvious that I did not fit the corporate mold. My chosen career didn't align with my true purpose and, deep down, I knew it. I despised the politics, had little talent for it, and chaffed at bureaucracy. I resented pressures against living my healthy lifestyle, an imposition that I addressed with years of sneaking off for lunchtime to avoid being detected by the muckety-mucks. Early on, a little voice inside began to whisper, "This is not what you were created for."

Not knowing what else to do, I kept on the corporate path. I tried different jobs in different companies, but by the late '90s I realized that I wanted out. To what exactly, I did not know. Just to a life that felt right. During that time, one of my favorite TV shows was HGTV's *The Good Life*, which featured people who had left traditional careers to start their own companies and live on their own terms. I admired these people and began to ask, "How could I do that?" My mindset at the time blocked me from hearing the answer, but the desire brewing inside was growing stronger.

It was difficult to see beyond a corporate career. This was all I'd known in life to date. Even my sense of self was heavily vested in corporate success, especially when reinforced by compliments that appealed to my ego's need to appear "successful."

Still, I couldn't deny the instinct pounding within that signaled I was out of alignment with my real purpose. I was starting to feel very uncomfortable and out of place in the corporate setting, yet remained ignorant about how to leave it. I simply did not have the spiritual and emotional maturity as yet to realize that all that was required for this change was a simple decision to leave.

I must have been moving too slowly for Spirit's taste because the pressure to change cranked up during the second decade of my career. I was increasingly well-compensated with a six figure income and enjoying significant responsibility, but several years in a couple of bureaucratic and political corporate cultures finally wore my spirit down. My passion faded and my results started to suffer. This way of life just didn't fit me anymore.

These years were emotionally painful, but they were a blessing. Experiencing extreme frustration motivated me to seek my true purpose with zeal, and finally, to pursue it. I surrendered to a series of significant life changes that required new levels of courage and conviction. The first was moving to Colorado, a place I loved and had dreamed of living in for years. The second was taking a step toward entrepreneurship by finding work with a dynamic small company after working for giants my entire career, even taking a significant pay cut to pursue the job.

A few of my big company colleagues reacted with raised eyebrows, but most expressed admiration at the boldness of my decisions. For me these moves represented real spiritual growth. They were big life decisions made from a place of faith that signaled to the Universe that I was serious about discovering and living my purpose. In fact, the decisions ignited a spiritual renaissance from which there was no return.

Two years of long hours and high stress at the small company ended in a layoff. As the sole wage earner for a family of five, with my livelihood suddenly removed, I would just have to find another job. At first that's what I thought. That's what everyone thought. But prior to the layoff I was already deeply engaged in a campaign of self-discovery and action that resulted in training for a coaching career and the business plan for two companies. When the layoff came, I was able to see through the fog of the previous two decades and embrace that I now had the perfect opportunity to make a new choice.

To everyone's surprise, I announced that I wouldn't be seeking another job. I decided instead to enter the ranks of solo-entrepreneurs and start my own business. It took all the courage and faith I could muster to take that first step, and I was both exhilarated and terrified. I had wrenching doubts about my ability to create a successful business from scratch, but somehow I took that first step… and then another. That's all that was needed: the courage and faith to take one step at a time. The rest – well, I relied on faith that this was my intended path and entrusted the details to God.

Once I truly committed, the synchronicities began. Kindred spirits came out of the woodwork. Resources and opportunities for growth arrived as they were needed. My spiritual growth continued to accelerate and I became increasingly comfortable pushing beyond my comfort zone on an almost daily basis. In making a commitment to this entrepreneurial path, I finally embraced my life's true work – the work that today fills my days with both passion and purpose.

This new path also chipped away at the chronic challenges of fear and low self-confidence that plagued me for decades. It's fair to say that I was reborn as the real me. The person hidden for years behind these challenges finally re-emerged into the light of day.

I'm amazed looking back because my life is so different now. Today I enjoy purpose-filled days in a business of my own that enables me to help others create purpose-filled lives through their own conscious businesses. I don't even feel like I work anymore, really, because what I've chosen to do with my time feels more like play.

My journey taught me that God will work perfectly in our lives if you bring but one grace to the table: desire. The journey required traveling a rocky road filled with my own fears and doubts to arrive at clarity about how I wanted to live, but my desire carried me through until I was able to embrace my true life and make an unshakable commitment to living it. From there it was a matter of mustering the courage to jump in with full faith that Spirit would be there to catch me.

I also came to know that if you crave your best life, your purpose will seek you. At times we might be too busy, afraid, or distracted with the rest of life to hear our purpose calling. But if you show just an ounce of desire to live that purpose, the Universe will work like water to wither away the stone of whatever stands between you and its fulfillment.

Julio Blanco is the founder of Envision Lifeworks, a company devoted to empowering solo-entrepreneurs with mindset and marketing practices that enable them to create a thriving business doing the work they love in a life they love. He mentors entrepreneurs through his RiverFlow Prosperity Program and the Perspectives on Marketing & Prosperity Blog (www.EnvisionLifeworksBlog. com). To learn more about Julio and obtain your Free report 12 Solopreneur Traps and How to Avoid Them, visit www.EnvisionLifeworks.com.

I Am Experiencing "N.O.W." - (New Omnipotent Ways)

~⟳

Susan M. Hampton

Two days before Christmas of 2008, my husband and I found out that the mortgage company had denied the loan modification we had hoped for. We had just completed nine months of a successful verbal forbearance program, and had hoped that this would then allow us to adjust our mortgage (which would have worked better financially for us), during the midst of the recession.

My stinkin' thinkin' wanted to wreak havoc on my life, yet God's voice kept reassuring me that we would be able to stay in our home. After the first of the year, in 2009, I was slapped in the face with the experience of seeing a couple who were living in a tent outside of a local church. I had heard that others were also living in tents in our community after losing their homes during these rough economic times. I decided to find a solution. It was then that I realized I needed to start using the tools that God had inspired me to share with others, back in March of 2008. I kept telling myself that I was a certified life empowerment coach, for heaven's sake, so "walk your talk, Susan!"

In March of 2008, I came across an affirmation that goes like this: "I am experiencing now the constant flow of prosperity and abundance." I was saying this phrase frequently to myself and had actually printed it off to have a constant visual reminder to attach to the dashboard of my car. So, when doing some errands one day, I had one of those "ah-ha" moments. It was like a bolt of lightning had struck me. The thought came to me that "**N.O.W.**" could be a reminder for me of "**New Omnipotent Ways**," as in almighty, absolute, infinite, or unlimited power.

With "**N.O.W.**" standing for "**New Omnipotent Ways**," I thought to myself that the only time I ever spoke or sang the word "omnipotent" in my life, was when singing a verse in Handel's Messiah with my school chorus that said, "For the Lord God omnipotent reigneth... Hallelujah, Hallelujah!"

Then I realized that omnipotent described God for me, and it was really *God's* constant flow of prosperity and abundance that filled my life, since He's directing this movie anyway!

In the past, I had been taught to express my affirmations in ways such as, "I am so happy now that _____," and then I filled in the blank with whatever I was believing - as if it were already happening in my life.

Well, I'm here to tell you that those types of affirmations didn't do much for me. What was revealed to me through this new insightful affirmation was the fact that when I thought about and/or said, "I am *experiencing* "N.O.W"....," it made me feel the feelings and emotions as if I were experiencing (in this case) God's constant flow of prosperity and abundance in the NOW - in the current moment.

If I used the old way of thinking, saying, "I am so happy now that I have prosperity and abundance in my life," it didn't connect my feelings with my thoughts. It was as if I had to practice the old "Fake it 'til I make it" way of thinking. You see, when I said, "I am so happy now that....," it was like I was trying to talk myself into the fact that I was happy about something in the future - something that I didn't believe was going to happen, as there was no feeling connected with the words.

When I had that "ah-ha" moment, I realized that if I said, "I am experiencing N.O.W....," I actually **felt** like I was being and/or doing the thing that followed it. This gave me more than the feelings of simply being "happy now." It actually exhilarated me! To experience new, power-filled ways of doing and being, now that was giving me authentic feelings of joy, without even trying to fake being happy now!

Before you go any further, do yourself a favor and experience **"N.O.W."** for yourself! Go ahead! Create an affirmation for you! One that is truly **you**!

Here, I'll help you out - you fill in the blank: "I am experiencing "N.O.W" (**n**ew **o**mnipotent **w**ays of) God's constant flow of
_____."

Now stand up and say this affirmation several times over, with feelings and emotions behind the words! Add some movement or perhaps some hand gestures that you normally do when you are excited.

Just feel the infinite possibilities of having, being, and doing what you want in your life! What thoughts are coming into your mind? What are you REALLY feeling?

Can you think of a time in your life when you had *similar* feelings of joy and success? Do yourself a favor and capture that moment, remembering those feelings and your emotions. Whenever you do your affirmations, focus on those same feelings and emotions, to *attract* what you are affirming. You will *attract* people and things that you resonate with because you are a spiritual being, in a physical body that has energetic and magnetic frequencies. Keep in mind - you were made in God's image.

Someone once told me that "Our lives are God's gift to us. What we do with our lives is our gift to God." This leads me to another tip that I'll share with you that's been really helpful for me. I once had a friend in the "AA" twelve-step program who taught me to say, "Let Thy will be done," and to say it fifty million times a day if I had to. I learned from my own experience that when I aligned my will with God's will, the results usually came out being better than I could have imagined. In fact, during the time in my life when I first started using this tool, I was fired from my job, later having it offered back to me with a pay raise. Around the same time, after the auto company's tow truck repossessed my car, I was able to get it back for half of what I owed on it. The icing on the cake was that rather than losing the place where I lived, I got a roommate who helped me to stay there by chipping in financially. My job, car, and my home all ended up bringing better results into my life than I could have ever imagined, all from using the phrase, "Let Thy will be done." Try it for a while, and see what happens in your life, when you align your will with *God's* will and desires for you.

What I've shared with you are just two tips that have worked for me, bringing success in my life. In fact, remember the loan modification that our mortgage company had denied for us, just two days before Christmas in 2008? Well, after using the two tips that I shared with you, exactly two months from the day we were denied, a representative from the mortgage company called us to tell us they wanted to overnight us papers to sign, with an offer that would reduce our interest rate by about 4% for the next five years, thus bringing our monthly payment down. Who would have thought that they would have been calling us to make us an offer, after denying us just two months before?

The improved mortgage program was not the only positive thing that happened after the first of the year. While taking action to learn what I could do to be able to offer group coaching - so I could inspire, empower, and motivate more people at a time - I started listening to teleseminars and BlogTalk radio, as well as watching webinars, to see what the people were doing who were already successfully getting their message out to large groups of people.

I was also being reminded by our seven and a half year old daughter that we needed to focus on what we wanted, instead of what we didn't want. (Can you tell she loves to watch "*The Secret*" DVD?) Each month I *attracted* a mentor or coach who taught me through webinars and teleclasses what I needed to know, to move my life coach business forward. It was amazing how they just all kept showing up at the right and perfect time, as if they were part of God's divine plan.

Even though my financial challenges had caused extreme stress in my life, those same challenges led me to positive opportunities, when I applied the solutions.

If you are currently struggling with your finances or life, use these tools daily to experience results beyond your imagination:

- Create, speak, and *feel* your new affirmations – I am *experiencing* "*N.O.W.*" God's constant flow of _____.

- Spend a few minutes in quiet time, aligning your will with *God's* will.

Repeatedly think and/or say throughout each day, "Let Thy will be done."

Now go experience success, fun, fulfillment, and a sense of freedom in your life today!

Susan M. Hampton *has a passion for empowering people to discover New Omnipotent Ways for achieving their success, fun, fulfillment, and a sense of freedom. Her clients say she has an amazing gift of inspiring others to experience breakthroughs, which lead to immediate solutions in their lives. Get a Free sneak peek of a chapter of Susan's upcoming book about the Law of Attraction from a Biblical perspective, when you subscribe to her* Experiencing N.O.W. *e-letter updates at www.NewOmnipotentWays.com.*

Getting Older (and Over!)
The "Not Enough" Syndrome

Marlene Oulton

As I examined the "laugh lines" surrounding my still baby blue eyes the other day, I thanked God for letting me live long enough to overcome what I call the "Not Enough" Syndrome. Most of us have been affected by this self-confidence squasher at some point in our lives. The "Not Enough" Syndrome covers a myriad of ills, and a few telltale symptoms are as follows: not being pretty "enough," smart "enough," thin "enough," tall "enough," or not worthy "enough" are just a few I have personally experienced. I am by no means a psychologist, therapist, or formally licensed "anything-ist," but I do know that having defeated the "Not Enough" Syndrome qualifies me to offer my remedies for beating this mind-altering malaise.

The "Not Pretty Enough" Syndrome Rears Its Ugly Head
I was the third child, and the only girl of four, born to hard-working, decent parents, who lived in a very rural village in New Brunswick, Canada. I thought I was just your average typical little girl... until I hit the age of ten and overheard a conversation that planted a painful seed

in my brain that remained firmly rooted for the next thirty-five years of my life.

In the summertime, our eighteen room rambling farmhouse became the "vacation spot" hotel for relatives from both sides of the family. One particular summer, two of my mother's sisters and respective children came to visit as per their usual practice. While entering into the kitchen through the back porch one afternoon, I heard one of my aunts say, "Marlene is such a helpful little girl. It's too bad she's so homely." Hmm… so I wasn't pretty. Pity. Now forty plus years later what do I believe? That beauty really does lie in the eye of the beholder, and true beauty lies within a person, not in the exterior covering we get to wear for our life on earth.

"Not Smart Enough" Syndrome Makes An Appearance

My oldest brother happened to be a whiz at most of his school studies. He excelled in Math and though he barely passed English, he still set a high standard for the rest of us siblings to meet. Having two parents who were both perfectionists didn't help much either, as I was always trying to please one or the other and never succeeding at pleasing them both simultaneously.

In Grade school and Junior High, I consistently scored the second highest marks in my class, but once I hit High School my marks started to take a turn for the worse, with one course exception – English. I loved the written word! I'd hide out in a corner of our huge house and read for hours on end, until either I finished the entire book or my Mom found me and made me go do chores! Reading was considered a useless pastime in our house unless one was perusing the latest farmer's article on how to grow better beans or repair a broken piston on a Massey Ferguson tractor.

I vividly recall bringing home a Grade 12 English term paper on which I'd received an A minus. My father responded, "Why didn't you get an A+?" while the whiz kid brother responded, "English doesn't really count anyway. Any stupid fool could pass that class." Ahh, so now I'm not only homely, I'm stupid. Blow number two struck by the "Not Enough" Syndrome. I'm now eternally grateful to all the authors of those books I devoured. If I'd not developed a love of words, I most likely wouldn't have the absolutely delicious company and job I treasure today.

"Not Worthy Enough" Almost Causes Hearing Loss

When I reached nineteen, my father sat me down one evening and informed me that I'd best find a job, as he had no intention of keeping me until I qualified for the Old Age pension. Having no great aspirations or callings at the time, I moved out of our rural community and went to live with my whiz kid brother and his family in a large city three hours away.

I found a job as a keypunch operator (now called data entry operator) with a large oil processing company. These were the days before keyboards made virtually no noise when you touched them, and computers then were the size of a 4' x 6' room! Every day a large buzzer would go off exactly at 12:00 noon and would sound again at 1:00 pm signaling the beginning and end of lunch hour. That one hour of silence was truly golden!

I detested that job! Being stuck in that room from 8:00 am – 5:00 pm, with only two short fifteen minute breaks and an hour for lunch and making the princely sum of $ 185.00 net every fifteen days was not what I had envisioned for my future. But… I wasn't "worthy" of anything better. With no formal college education, what else could I do? Besides, I had to work at something and this mind-numbing, deafening job just reinforced my "not smart enough" symptoms. Looking back, I realize that I allowed those feelings of unworthiness to rent space in my head. Today, I only allow good people and great, positive thoughts to reside in my grey matter. I'd rather fill that space up with love than with refuse from years gone by.

Enter the "You're Not Good Enough to Be With" Stage

I'll keep this stage short and sweet because I'm going to write a full length novel about these two and a half decades when I retire. Suffice it to say that I married the first man who asked me because I was fairly certain I wasn't "good enough" wife material, so best say yes to the first half-decent man who proposed. We parted ways after three and a half years and I didn't get to keep the washer and dryer in the settlement. Bummer.

Marriage number two occurred when I was twenty-seven and I believed he was my knight in shining armor who rode in on a white horse to rescue me. Turned out the armor was rusty and his horse was really a mule in disguise. That marriage almost made it to eight years before I found myself in the single scene again. And AGAIN I didn't get to keep the washer and dryer. Of course, the reason why none of these marriages lasted was because I wasn't "good enough" a wife. Where was Martha Stewart when I needed her?

The best counterpart to the "Not Good Enough" Syndrome is this quote I discovered about ten years ago by Eleanor Roosevelt, who said, "No one can make you feel inferior without your consent." Write this down in your journals, laminate it, paint it on your walls – do whatever you need to do to remember those words because they will allow you to take everything you hear, see, or read about yourself with a grain of salt.

"Here Come the 40's"... thankfully!

I cannot tell you how relieved I was to reach my fortieth birthday! I celebrated that birthday with only one goal for that decade – to find out what and when is 'enough' enough.

I started to read self-help books by wonderfully wise authors such as Melodie Beattie, *Co-Dependent No More: How to Stop Controlling Others and Start Caring for Yourself*, Sarah Ban Breathnach's *Simple Abundance Journal of Gratitude*, and a numerous host of others. I determined that it was high time I became better acquainted with this lady I saw in the mirror. After forty years of existing, I needed to understand why I was here and start living.

Getting Older (and Over!) The "Not Enough" Syndrome

Shortly before my 49th birthday I decided to boldly go where many had dared to go before me and become an entrepreneur. On April 15, 2006, my company, Write Choice Virtual Assistants, was born. I had tons of administrative experience to draw upon and based my services on these skill sets. Yet in the back of my mind I kept thinking, "You know, I really love to write and proofread. Wouldn't it be cool if I could manage to get some work along those lines?"

By this time the Universe, God, and I had formed a formidable triangle of mutual respect and love, so I shouldn't have been surprised when requests to proofread/edit and write articles, ebooks, website content etc. started to flow into my inbox. I had finally become "enough."

I have now redefined "enough" in my world today as follows:

- If I treat people with love, kindness and respect, that is "enough."

- If I have a roof over my head, clothes on my back, and food on my table, that is "enough."

- If I can help another human being on this journey called life, that is "enough."

- If I do my work conscientiously, with care and love, that is "enough."

- If I am at peace with and within myself, that is "enough."

May you be more "enough" than you ever imagined possible!

Marlene Oulton, *resident wordsmith/editor of Write Choice Virtual Assistants and BulletProofers.com derives great satisfaction from assisting authors, writers, coaches, and entrepreneurs to produce clean, crisp, and concisely written articles, newsletters, website copy, and other literary works. Known as* The Words Lady *by her clients and friends, her articles can be found on various online article sites. Visit www.BulletProofers.com and www.WriteChoiceVA.com to find out more on how she can make your words sing and dance... without adding music!*

Create a Magical Life:
Tap into Your Soul's Intention
of Abundance

Catherine Newton

Ever since I was a little girl, I believed in fairytales. My favorite story-book character was Tinker Bell. I loved her wand and how she would sprinkle magic fairy dust wherever she went. So, as any child would, I did the same. And all, it seems, for a reason...I was blessed with an innocently happy childhood, scattered, much like the Disney stories I read, with its share of dramas and happy endings. My father was absent almost from the beginning and finally left when I was two. My mother was forced to get a job to support my sister and me, putting us into daycare, which in the early 70's was unheard of. When I was six, my mother remarried, and had two children with my step-father. By the time I was eleven, he too was gone. At this stage I had two brothers, ages one and three, along with my sister. Once again Mom had to go back to work, only this time I was old enough to be responsible for helping her with my siblings. I would help Mom cook for them, change their diapers, entertain them, and be there for them like any "Mom" would, all from the age of twelve. While my friends had a father in their lives, I watched my Mother juggle being both Mom and Dad, nurturer and provider.

Our Experiences Shape Us Into Who We Become

Isn't it those lessons in life that teach you what you do and don't want? I learned from an early age what I wanted. I had read enough fairytales to know that I wanted my life to flow, to be surrounded with abundance, and for my soul mate to stay. As far as I was concerned I didn't want to be on my own or to worry about money. And so out would come my magic wand with its fairy dust and I would wish away.

And so it happened. At the tender age of seventeen I met my very own Elf... called Alf! By twenty-one I was married. Here was someone who would take care of me, provide for the family we would have, and whisk me off on great adventures. All my dreams had come true and I felt blessed. My magic wand had worked.

Just When Life Seems All "Tickety-boo"...

Skip forward nineteen years and now I see life with a new perspective. Out came a magic wand bigger than mine and whipped the sprinkles out from under me. I thought I had the perfect life – every little girl's dream. I was quite content with life. I wasn't at my fullest potential, but I was comfortable and wanted for nothing. Or so I thought...

It's hard to know what went wrong. We had a "good enough" marriage, but as the years ticked by we simply grew apart. It was as if the Universe knew that as I stepped into my Purpose, this fairy dream no longer served me. So, in came "life" with a big wrench and pried us apart. Gradually, amicably, we began to go our separate ways.

Holding Onto That Rock Solid Faith

As I felt my marriage falling apart I knew I needed my magic wand more than ever. In my mind I would picture the fairy dust pouring onto me, protecting and guiding me. I held on to a rock solid faith that everything would be okay. I felt fully supported by the Universe and I knew everything was happening for a greater reason.

But have you ever tried hanging on to that trust when your castle is being crumbled? Boy, it's challenging, to say the least, but hang on I did! There was a voice inside me that kept telling me all would be well. My job was simply to trust and let my destiny and Universe do their job.

With my marriage over and my dignity intact, I knew that every minute of trusting had been worth it. But just how worth it only Tinker Bell could have guessed! My life was about to unfold in the most miraculous way...

The Importance of Listening to Your Intuition

2 months after my marriage ended, I attended a reunion. I deliberated whether to go. I knew Alf would be there plus all our mutual friends. It would be our first "outing" since separating and I wasn't sure I was ready.

My inner voice was screaming at me to go, so I listened and decided to attend. I made every effort to look great that night and as I drove the two and a half hours to the reunion, I called up every smattering of magic dust I could visualize and I mentally showered myself with it.

Before I walked into the venue I took a moment to further prepare myself. Part of me was SO nervous, but I knew I had to do this. I had to get over my fear, step into that room, and embrace the moment. So I called in my power, (the one that makes me feel like I can do anything), and set the intention that this evening would go well. Then in I went.

I had an "on top of the world" feeling as the evening progressed. My magic dust was working overtime and when a girlfriend suggested we slip out for a drink, I jumped at the opportunity. I was so proud of myself for facing my fears that I was ready to celebrate.

How the Universe Conspired

As we entered the bar it was then I knew that all the events of my life had conspired for this moment. You see, one week previously I had written a wish list for my ideal man. I had written down everything I wanted in a soul mate. I really believed he was coming and visualized him in my life; then I passed my magic wand over it and let the Universe do its job.

Life "happened" to us without giving us any say in that moment. The minute Jason and I saw each other it was as if nothing else existed in the room except each other. As we were introduced my heart and my soul was screaming, "It's him!" And as the night wore on and we shared our first romantic sunrise together, I knew my heart was right.

Finding Jason has given me such joy. Even as I write this I am filled with a sense of fulfillment and gratefulness that the synchronicities of the evening led us to meet. But there is a deeper reason at force here. The night I met him was just one event that has given meaning to my abundant life.

Seeing the Reason

In her book "*Everything Happens for a Reason,*" Mira Kirshenbaum writes, "The good that comes out of the bad things that happen to you is to help you become your best authentic self." We think we know what's right for us, then an event happens in our life and we are presented with huge lessons to learn. With every situation that happened in my life I knew it was not the event itself that mattered, but the way I handled it that counted. When my marriage was disintegrating, rather than freaking out, I continually asked myself, "What is there to learn from this?" I soon developed a sense that everything does indeed happen for a reason and with my magic wand I am well looked after.

If I hadn't gone through what I did in my life I wouldn't be the person I am today. If my life had been perfect, I wouldn't have learned the tools that have helped me step up to this greatness that now envelops my life. I wouldn't have found my purpose, stepped up into my path and found my true abundance. And so for all the experiences, good or otherwise, that have, and will come my way, I am so grateful.

What it Takes to Be Your Authentic Self

Empower yourself with these ten steps and you will be unstoppable:

- Use your magic wand and **allow** magic light to flow into you, from your Divine Source.

- **Create** the outcome you desire. **Ask** for what you want, not with desperation, but from the feeling of fulfillment.

- Visualize that place of power within you and step into the immense feeling of **believing** that you can do it.

- Meditate regularly, taking time to **receive** the positive outcome.

- Take the necessary **action** toward helping your desires become reality.

- Use **affirmations** to inspire you.

- **Trust** that the Universe is conspiring towards what's best for you, having rock solid **faith** that all will be well.

- **Celebrate** the outcome, showing the Universe how **grateful** you are.

- Realize that **everything happens for a reason** and it's not what happens, but how you deal with it that matters.

The abundance that is your birthright can now flow easily to you!

Catherine Newton *is a Wealth and Abundance Coach and Law of Attraction Expert who can show you step-by-step how to intentionally create Wealth and Abundance in your life. To find out how you can be unstoppable, allowing you to let in the abundance that you really desire, claim your special Free audio report,* How to Intentionally Create All the Abundance You Need, *at www.CatherineNewton.com and start your soul intentions towards abundance now.*

COURAGE

Courage is being scared to death - but saddling up anyway.
~ JOHN WAYNE

The Awesome Power of Optimism: A Personal Journey to HOPE

Frances Thomas

My story is not a "rags to riches" account, it's about surviving with the "rags" that you have. It's about finding the "unique you," even when your mind/body/soul imprint seems understood only by God. It's about anchoring your "spirit" to the belief that God doesn't make junk, training your "mind" to be positive, even when the situations that the "body" faces are negative and unfair. My story is for the everyday people who have to sustain the courage to face crisis after crisis because of immovable obstacles and long-suffering conditions. Nothing comes easily; it's analogous to always traveling rough terrain. Welcome to life on the rough side of the mountain. My life's journey represents the upward climb, as that was the only direction forward.

My name is not recognized for its greatness. My circle of influence was rather local, but my impact has been profound and broad. I am an ordinary person who through faith and hard work found HOPE, and now devotes my life to the multitudes of people who need to find it. I was born a poor, skinny, nearly blind, dark-complexioned Afro-American girl, prior to school desegregation, equitable public transportation and accommodations. If we were measuring these barriers to success on a one to ten scale, my failure indicator would be seven. Add one more for the emotional torture that I endured from the age of three because my eyeglasses were so thick and heavy. Add another point because I was stereotyped when transferred as a Kindergartener to special education due to being unable to keep up with the pace of a regular classroom. Point ten is appropriate because I had to travel on three buses everyday across the city to that segregated, low vision program that could meet my needs. Finally, add one more point for being a marginalized citizen trying to reap the benefits of the American dream. Wow! That's eleven on a scale of one to ten. I hope my story speaks to all whose immovable walls are their body image, social or cultural constraints - things that you can't make disappear, but which you don't have to allow to stymie or entrap you. Sometimes you have to find the capacity to create the new from nothing.

I am now a self-actualized sixty-seven year old college graduate in private practice as a spiritual stress management therapist and life coach. I have taught at three universities, mentored thousands during my forty-five year professional tenure, and count life as a blessed journey, still well worth the efforts. As I look back, I have several encouraging vignettes that I want to share, because if I can get through it - you can!

The will to press forward in spite of circumstances is a choice between survival and victimization. Never seeing myself as a victim, I forged ahead and grew through adversity. My years in special education taught me to look for strength in people beyond their broken images or outward labels. They were the preparatory experiences that led me to become uniquely non-judgmental. People seemed drawn to my calmness. I was just trying to get the most out of my opportunities. My limited sight and dark skin seriously restricted labor job options, so as my way out of the ghetto, I dared to be the first one in my family to attend college, only to be de-railed with another detour. My plan was junior college, then getting credentialed to teach, but I was not allowed to declare that major because I couldn't pass the physical. This blow was detrimental, considering that my parents didn't have a dime to contribute toward my education, so the state supported program had seemed most achievable. But now even that was not feasible.

"Keep climbing up the mountain, there's got to be a solution," I kept telling myself. There was a way - a full scholarship to a well-known four-year university program from a sorority that was soliciting members with high grade point averages. **Advice to my readers: make the most of the gifts that you have; sometimes you have more than you think going for you.** By now it was becoming clear to me that I was headed on an anointed path if I just stayed on the course. Optimism was my spiritual gift.

I received a BS degree upon graduation, but what to do specifically with minors in psychology, sociology, and ethics? What about finances? I was praying to find my niche where I could empower people, because in my struggles I noticed how pessimism so often overpowered optimism. I was led to social work and accepted in a work-study position at a major hospital, qualified for a community health stipend, and enrolled in an MSW program.

At this point in my life I was getting used to things always being difficult, but I was not prepared for the bigotry that I faced with an instructor who told me that under no circumstances should I, an African American, expect an "A" grade. Optimism doesn't expect perfection, but also doesn't acknowledge failure. Thanks to God and personal determination, I successfully managed to carry twenty-one credit hours, work forty hours per week, while not being able to drive due to my eyesight. **Readers: label life's challenges as motivating calls to positive actions, not to anger or false pride. You might find that you can accomplish the improbable.**

Education now completed, next step should be family, but remember, I reside on the rough side of the mountain. My second son, whom I was so happy to conceive since I had prayed to raise two children of the same sex, was regretfully born with a rare congenital heart condition. He had a life expectancy of eighteen months. How do you prepare for that? Add that burden to the demands of a care-giving career where your peak is expected, regardless of your personal dilemmas. I held on to my faith and Optimism pushed us both forward to be heroic positive role models. God renewed my son's "life contract" for thirty-one years. Our "be the best that you can be" philosophy empowered him to be a dedicated husband and father, in addition to being disabled. Though forever wounded by the grief of his death in 2004, I emerged even more resilient, and am now imparting that drive to the grandchildren and all who will listen.

Remember, my story is for those who have to operate like the little fire engine whose might was based on the attitude of, "I think I can," because the challenges never stop coming. As I mentioned, near blindness has always been my cross to bear. It's amazing how people take vision for granted, but just close your eyes and imagine the impact of blindness. I have undergone four eye surgeries with no guarantees, but Optimism is fearless. At age forty, I was able to pass the motor vehicle eye examination and drive for the first time because technology had produced new tri-focal featherweight eyeglasses. That new lease on life is now being threatened by scar tissue build up, but again, Optimism is relentless. Now that I am a semi-retired senior, I'll just live as much of my life during daylight hours as possible and avoid night driving. **Readers: don't minimize your threats: develop survival strategies before you need them. You can manage stress - it doesn't have to manage you.**

I am thankful for the opportunity to do this life review, but more hopeful that my stories of everyday survival give courage and fortitude to those who might doubt the value of the struggle. All things do come together for good, if you value each linked experience as the strength of your life chain. This is so important to know for yourself because the challenges that continue to present themselves might well not be deserved. This statement brings me to the present. Just when I thought I understood the rhythm of survival on the rough side of the mountain, I almost fell off. One year before I would have reached full retirement age, my job was terminated. After thirty-three years of dedication and excellence, I was in the way. What does an elderly, near blind sole supporter do now? There was no comfortable buy-out, just eight weeks of severance and no health insurance. The circumstances were even threatening my longtime dream of closure through an official retirement celebration. My failure indicator score was going back up again, but by now I know who I am - a conqueror, valued by God. He keeps the final score. With the help of a dear colleague and friend, I enjoyed a momentous exit, and have comfortably re-rooted. **Readers: Optimism is an expression of God's Omnipotence: never give up, even when you have to give in. Keep climbing forward. HOPE is there.**

In this current wave of economic and social crisis, many are traveling on the same side of the mountain where I live. I say to you: anchor yourself in the belief that God cares, but find the strength to keep climbing. **Optimism is your guide and will not lead you to failure.**

Frances J Thomas, MSW, LCSW is a devoted mother, grandmother, and mentor to many. She maintains a busy private practice as a Spiritual Stress Management Therapist and Life Coach at Agape Christian Counseling in St. Louis, Missouri, where she grew up. Frances is active in her church and community, especially enjoying singing and leading music.

Saying Good-bye to a Business I Loved

Christine Kloser

It was early 2006, after suffering a heartbreaking miscarriage, that I was faced with one of the biggest decisions of my life. I had been operating a business I loved for the past six years. However, after miscarrying, I went through a deep reevaluation of my life and my career. And I was beginning to sense it was time to shut down my business. The problem was that I loved it so much!

I had started this business in 2000, the Network for Empowering Women Entrepreneurs, out of my own need to connect with like-minded, spiritually oriented, entrepreneurial women. I was starved for these types of connections, but hadn't found them anywhere in Los Angeles in the already existing myriad of women's networking groups. Every networking event I went to left me feeling more empty, more lost, and more like I didn't fit in anywhere.

So, in April 2000, when I asked a few friends to meet with me on the first Thursday of the month for dinner and conversation about supporting each other in business, four of my friends showed up to join me. But none of them were entrepreneurs. I didn't KNOW any entrepreneurs at the time, but I knew I had to start somewhere.

To my surprise, when I showed up for dinner the next month in May 2000, none of my friends from the first meeting were there, but another five women showed up to join me for dinner... all friends of my friends who were at the first meeting.

And this was the beginning of what became the first ever women's networking group that blended spirituality and business. There was such a need for this type of group that, before I knew it, the small dinner gathering grew to seventy-five women, and there were five hundred members throughout the country. I started this small dinner group with no expectation of it being anything more than perhaps ten of us meeting every month, supporting each other in our businesses and in our lives.

Needless to say, I was not prepared for the rapid, organic growth the Network for Empowering Women Entrepreneurs encountered. Heck, I didn't have any intention of it being a business in the first place - it was just supposed to be a support group for me and a few other women entrepreneurs.

The fact that I managed to keep it running for six years was a minor miracle. I hadn't built the business on a profit model that made any financial sense. I subsidized its operating costs by starting a seminar division and a book publishing division, but the organization in and of itself was losing money very early on.

I stuck with it because I absolutely loved the women who had become members. I felt like I stepped into my power as a woman, an entrepreneur, a leader, and a teacher by running this organization. It was my identity. It fed my soul on such a deep and much needed level; the fulfillment it brought me was like nothing I'd ever experienced in my life. Literally, our monthly meetings were like a "love fest" of powerful, spiritual women entrepreneurs. Businesses grew, success stories abounded, friendships deepened, and a community flourished.

Then, in February 2005, at the height of the organization's growth, my husband and I joyfully welcomed our first child, and soon decided we wanted to move from Los Angeles to the East Coast to be closer to my parents, both of our siblings, and our daughter's cousins. It was the right decision for us as a family, but I knew it would have a huge impact on the Network for Empowering Women Entrepreneurs, as the organization had been built around my presence and leadership.

By the summer of 2005, after being out of Los Angeles for a few months, I had a sense that I wouldn't be able to keep running the business from afar, and I wasn't going to be moving back to Los Angeles anytime soon. But due to the passion, love, and fulfillment this organization still brought me, its hundreds of members and thousands of newsletter subscribers, I didn't feel I could let it go. I had to figure out how to keep it going, even if it drained me financially. How could I let down my members? How could I shut down a business that brought so much good to so many women? How could I stop providing a service that was so needed? How could I let go of one of the best experiences in my life?

These were the questions I kept asking myself over and over again, and I could never come up with an answer other than "I couldn't." Deep down inside, I knew I had to shut down the business from a financial perspective, but I couldn't bring myself to do it. So, I kept losing money month after month because I just couldn't let anyone down.

This fear of letting other people down and not paying attention to my own needs were very familiar default behaviors for me. I was always the peace maker, very careful to make sure everyone was happy, even if it meant sacrificing my own needs and happiness.

But after my miscarriage in 2006 (on the day after Christmas), something inside of me began to change. I started asking myself deeper questions. I wondered if it was really worth it for me to keep losing money on a business that I knew I would never be able to turn around financially. I began to realize that perhaps the pain it caused me financially wasn't worth it, and it was time to make the right decision for me.

Less than eight weeks after my miscarriage, I also decided that it wasn't worth the stress to try to keep the business operating. It was challenging enough managing my post-miscarriage emotions. I realized that even though I loved my Network for Empowering Women Entrepreneurs members very much, I had to love myself more and make the right decision for me.

Making the decision to release the organization was very challenging. I can still remember the tears that fell as I wrote the emails to the members to inform them that I'd be closing down the organization. Hitting the "send" button on those emails created an experience of deep sorrow and sadness for the end of something that was so fulfilling to my soul, and also an experience of deep relief, as I'd no longer be losing money every month just trying to keep the business afloat.

I honestly believe that even though my miscarriage was one of the most painful experiences I've been through, it was also a gift that helped me overcome my fear of letting other people down; my fear of what people would think about me if my business failed; my fear of what I would think of myself after having a public failure such as this one; and my fear that I just didn't have what it takes to succeed.

Little did I know at the time I went through this that the choice I finally made to shut down the business was the very opening that's led to the success I'm experiencing in my business today. The most important thing I learned through this journey is that everything truly does happen for a reason. And it's up to me to look for the deeper meaning in my experiences and to be open to the gifts and the lessons that are sometimes wrapped in sadness and pain.

So, I invite you now to take a look at your life. First, allow yourself to notice if you're doing something (or not doing something) because you don't want to let other people down. If you can relate to this in your own life, take some time to journal about it to discover the gift that is trying to reveal itself to you.

Second, if you find yourself in a business situation where you feel like you've come to the end of a path... trust the saying that, "When one door closes, another door opens." This was certainly true for me, and I know that if you're going through a similar "letting go" in your business, that it's true for you, too. One door never closes unless another door is simultaneously opening. So, look for the openings and you'll be amazed at the opportunities just waiting for you to notice them.

Christine Kloser, best-selling author of The Freedom Formula, *teaches entrepreneurs how to put more soul in their business and more money in their bank, by taking a conscious approach to their business and their life. She is considered a leading pioneer in the field of conscious entrepreneurship and is a regularly featured expert in both online and offline media outlets. To get your FREE copy of Christine's* Conscious Business Success Kit, *visit www.LoveYourLife.com today.*

Surrender To The Moment

Holly Eburne

It is Monday, April 27th, 2009, and I just came back from the most incredible bike ride along our country road. The sun was bright, the air was crisp, and I could feel the peacefulness settling in as I listened to the sounds of nature. There were vireos and warblers singing and flitting among the dogwoods and a pair of majestic Great Blue herons "whooshing" as they flew out of the marshes. A little further along, there were the heavy hoof sounds as cows were being corralled into a cattle truck by real live cowboys and their border collies. It used to bring me to tears when I saw cows being loaded up for transfer, or when I would make eye contact with them through those narrows slits on the trucks when I passed them on the highway. I prefer to delude myself by thinking they are heading off to lush green pastures - sort of a bovine retirement home.

As the sun was warming the day, I noticed a long line of cows poking their heads out through weathered rails, eating hay. All those curly topped heads, wet noses the shape of triangles, and lovely, liquid-brown eyes. I have often wondered why these creatures affect me the way they do. Maybe it is their peaceful, soulful eyes which look directly at me, not above my head, or to the side looking at who might be passing them by. Perhaps it just feels good to witness their natural ability to surrender to their surroundings and life, making peace with whatever comes their way... just as I have.

For the past seventeen years I have cycled this road, yet I have never experienced such indescribable richness. When my husband, Dave, and I would go for a ride, we would be lucky to see one or two deer or coyotes, but today I realized that there is so much more. I had to slow down, clear the clutter in my brain, and allow myself to be "present" in the moment to truly see the beauty all around me.

Life hasn't always been this rich and fulfilling. Two years ago my husband, who had just turned fifty-seven, was diagnosed with Fronto-temporal Dementia, the second most common form of dementia in the younger group. It affects the front half of the brain, mainly personality, emotional, and language areas. When I watch Dave, who often has a vacant look on his face, struggling to read a sentence or trying to remember a cousin he has known since childhood, it is hard to believe he taught forestry in high school for twenty-five years. When Dave turned fifty-five, he was faced with early retirement. Every day he woke up with piercing headaches and was forgetting students' names and faces. Looking back, there were so many obvious signs of dementia, yet it was incredibly easy to blame all of them on stress!

I first met Dave thirty-five years ago outside the gym at the University of British Columbia, Canada. I was on the varsity curling and rowing teams and Dave was a star rugby player. You couldn't miss his 6'4", 225 lb. frame of pure muscle on or off the field. In the summer of '75, I had incredible luck when he turned out to be the head lifeguard at the pool where I was hired as the second guard. From the moment I saw him up close with those gorgeous blue eyes, I knew he was the man for me. There was such peacefulness and honesty about him. He didn't care that his jeans were five inches too short or that he wore white socks with his desert boots, or even that his coarse, wiry hair couldn't be tamed. He was the "real deal" and from the beginning I have never had to pretend to be someone else for him to be happy. What a rare gift! Dave has shown me the balance I needed. I grew up in a home where everything had to be in perfect order, all the time. Our Sunday clothes and hats were the latest styles, our cars were brand new, and the house was impeccable.

We have been married for thirty-one years on August 25th, 2009, and although we have had our share of arguments over money, kids, and messes, there has never been a day or moment when I questioned why I married him. When I was young, my Mom used to tell me that I had better marry a millionaire, as I had such expensive tastes, but when she met Dave she said, "Forget what I said about a millionaire. Grab this guy before someone else does!"

I have learned a lot from Dave, including how he handled the news in the neurologist's office in March 2007. He has this amazing ability to stay calm in stressful situations, whether it was with our kids during their baby "croup" years, or dealing with a chainsaw injury to one of his forestry students. His steady emotions balanced the sickening feeling in my gut when the doctor showed us the CT images of the blackened, damaged areas of Dave's brain, while asking us if we had our affairs in order.

I'm not sure if I could have faced his fate with such grace. Many times I have asked Dave if he has ever been angry or ashamed about his dementia and the answer is simple, and always the same... no. His only worry is for our children and he frets that he has passed this condition on to them. There is genetic testing for Frontotemporal dementia, but I am not quite ready to journey down that road.

One afternoon we were sitting on our deck listening to the spring birds and the air was filled with a wonderful sense of peace and calm.

Dave was lying back on his Adirondack chair and looking up at the sky, which has now become one of his favorite things to do. He pointed out a cloud that had two tails, and a minute later, the tail had become a head and was moving in the opposite direction. Boy, do I ever remember losing my patience with him three years ago when he would obsessively talk about the sky, the clouds, and the jet streams. It was so darn boring! Yet now, my perspective is different.

How many of us take the time to sit, like Dave, in silence, simply watching the sky float by, without a book in hand, and the TV, cell phone, and radio turned off? How many of us are curious enough to see animals in the clouds and to be entertained by jet streams fading away to nothing? I know little children are content to do this, but somewhere along our years, we lose ourselves to life. We become so busy, filling every moment with "stuff" and "shoulds" that we forget to take time out just to BE. Dave's dementia has taught me that life really can be simple and easy. I have often joked that living with him is like living with a four year old with a driver's license. A friend of mine wisely told me that it may seem exactly like that because he has the innocence and curiosity of a child, but he also brings his fifty-seven years of wisdom to our lives. I had forgotten that.

Honestly? Living with dementia hasn't been easy. There are many moments when I hate it - those times when I have to remind Dave to shower and change his clothes every few days; being responsible for the running of the entire household, including furnaces and washing machines that break down; and that I've lost a loving husband who used to cuddle and remember jokes. My family, friends, and life counselor have held my hand along this journey of awakening, and I will be forever grateful for their support and love. I am beginning to understand when they say, "You need darkness to see the stars."

Whenever I feel overwhelmed by life and wonder how I will manage, I take a bike ride along our country road or a quiet walk in the woods. I let my mind be silent and soak in the beauty all around me. At the end of every day, I write five things I am grateful for in a journal, which has helped me to see the hidden beauty in my darkness. And whenever I see those sweet, peaceful cows grazing in the farmer's field, I remember that life doesn't have to be a "race to the finish." It is simple and easy - if only I would let it BE.

Holly Eburne is a Physiotherapist and Health and Wellness Coach. She lives with her husband and their animals in Kamloops, British Columbia, Canada. To read more about Holly and Dave's journey, where they are discovering the enjoyment of life together despite their ever-changing world with dementia, visit www.HollyEburne.com. You will also receive a free report titled, Transforming a Moment- *Holly's simple 3 step formula for changing her sad and frustrating moments to ones of joy and understanding.*

How Big Is Your Tent? One Man's Quest to Find the Answer for More, More, More

Joshua Aragon

As I sat in my office contemplating what was occurring, I was overtaken by a mental and physical numbness. How could I have just sat by and let this happen? This was my ticket, my lifelong dream, and I let it slip right through my fingers. I put everything I was and had into making this business a success, and now everything was gone.

I didn't know it then, but I was being given a gift very early in my life, the greatest gift I have ever received, aside from life itself. I had come so close to achieving my dreams that I was willing to let everything else go in the pursuit, and in the end I lost everything. This is the story of how I moved from being a meaningless wanderer, to a fulfilled lover and teacher of life.

Starting at a very young age I can remember never feeling satisfied for long. For example, I once purchased a tent, large by tent standards, yet not large enough for my own. I would keep this tent for a few weeks until the newness wore off, and when it was no longer large enough, I would take it back to the store and exchange it for an even larger tent; one that I was sure I wouldn't grow tired of because it was even bigger than the last, had more rooms, windows, and doors. Of course, after two or three weeks, I was back at the store running through the same process yet again, promising myself this was the *one* without a doubt.

As I grew older this process repeated itself many times, only "things" just got larger and more complex than tents. No matter how much I attained, it was never enough and I always felt there was something better just around the corner. To most people looking at me from the outside, I was a great success and going places. On the inside, however, I was starting to feel as though I would never get what I wanted. The problem was, I didn't yet know what that was.

My habit of trading up and wanting more had hit a peak and the foundation of my life began to crumble in the months leading up to the big crash. I had lost three houses, three cars, a business, and my good credit rating, but it didn't stop there. Along with the disappearing material possessions went a great friend, a long time business partner, a marriage, and close relationships with family, friends, employees and others.

While these losses seem huge, they were inconsequential compared to those I was incurring within myself: loss of pride, trust, and confidence led to failure and helplessness. I failed, not only as an entrepreneur, but also as a friend, leader, husband, partner, and provider.

The final card to fall was the one that ultimately rocked my world more than anything else I had experienced. The business I had bet the world on, traded relationships, money, opportunities, freedom, and my soul for, had crashed. I had gone from building a $100 million a year business, and the fulfillment of my wildest dreams, to the depths of my worst nightmare. Everything I had identified myself with up to this point was gone. So who was I now without the titles, wealth, cars, houses, or my friends and family?

The first reality I had to face was that my career and love of being an entrepreneur was over, at least for now, and I had no choice but to find a job. The second was that I would have to move back in with my mother until I was able to get back on my feet financially and emotionally. And finally, I had to begin the process of healing, the first part of which included taking full responsibility for everything I had been through and had put others through.

The second part of putting my life back together started with the repair of key relationships, the most important of which being the relationship with myself, followed by those with God, my children, family and friends.

I then took the time to study just about anything I could get my hands on, in search of answers and help in putting my life back together. I attended countless seminars, read hundreds of books, consulted with mentors and coaches, spent time meditating, journaling, and doing dream work, along with many other forms of inquisition. I even ventured back into my past and started reviewing who I was as a child and teenager. What I found was not what I expected.

I discovered that what I had been searching for through much of my life, without being aware of it, was true meaning and fulfillment. I wanted to know that my life had a purpose and meant something to humanity. I also wanted to believe that on my death bed I wouldn't look back and discover that I had missed the whole purpose of my life, and I'd gotten it all wrong. Up to this point I had been trying to fill this hole in my soul with all of the things that brought me temporary joy, such as that of having a newer and bigger tent.

I also learned that everything that happened to me had a purpose and occurred right when it needed to. Events and conversations that at one point seemed commonplace now carried meaning and relevance. Consciously or unconsciously, I had started a chain of events that led to the business failure, and now I understood why.

This process opened me up to an awareness that everything I needed and desired to bring me true fulfillment was not only available to me, but it was within me, and had been there since I first arrived on this planet. It had just been waiting for the day when I would recognize my true nature and divinity, and reclaim the life which I was born to live. There was no amount of money, sex, houses, cars, jobs, tents or "things" that would ever quench my thirst and desire for true fulfillment. It was only in finding the path of my true purpose and living it, that the Universe would open up and show me the way home.

My journey has been remarkable - one which I continue to live and enjoy in wonder. I now have an amazing fiancée and five beautiful kids with whom I get to share in the joys of life. My career, after many successful years as an entrepreneur and leader in the technology industry, is nearing a close, to allow more time for me to pursue my writing, teaching and speaking. The process of reinventing my life was, and still is, both enlightening and synchronistic. Although the struggles still exist, (you should see my tent now!), I now have a new perspective from which to look at life.

It is my hope that by sharing some of the key lessons I have learned on this journey, you too, can benefit from their transformational attributes.

The first is to take responsibility for your life and know that you have the strength, power, and courage to deal with any situation in which you find yourself. Rather than placing the blame on others and rendering yourself powerless, know that you come from the Source of all and with it, there is nothing you cannot do or be.

The second is to know that no matter where you are in life, regardless of your age, present health, wealth, circumstances, or beliefs, nothing is permanent and you can change your life, starting right now. Become today the person who you were meant to be. It all becomes possible with just one thought.

The third lesson is that you were sent here to shine. Don't be afraid of what lies within the shadows. Know that it's good and never accept anything less than your own personal best. You're not in competition with others; you must only strive to make yourself better today than you were yesterday.

The final and perhaps most important lesson is to stop asking yourself, "What's in it for me?" and start each day by asking, "How may I serve?"

For me it took facing great material success (and loss), without fulfillment and meaning, to bring about the great shift that has occurred in my life. It took the realization that for the rest of my life I would always be chasing a goal that would never truly get me where I wanted to be, to place me on the path that I was meant to live.

My journey here is about helping others unlock their full potential and to see their true light. I hope that my story will give you the courage and inspiration to go forward and begin your own journey towards enlightenment, as you live your purpose and change the world... one "tent" at a time.

Offering both the wisdom of a teacher and the interest of a fellow learner, life purpose guide, and visionary teacher, **Joshua Aragon** *is passionate about enabling others to achieve their own dreams of success and make a lasting difference in the world. If you're ready to live a life worth living, a life of purpose and fulfillment, then visit www.JoshuaAragon.com to get a complimentary eCourse, 25 Secrets to Living a More Purposeful Life today.*

Calling of the Heart

~⟋⟍⟋

Nelie Johnson, MD

"I feel like quitting." What am I saying to myself? How can I quit the career I put nine years of university, medical school, and a year's internship to achieve? Not to mention the four years of supplemental training in hospitals in Britain and almost 10 years of family practice to this point in 1991. How can I be saying that to myself?

I couldn't have been more certain that I had a real calling for a career in medicine – helping people with their general health, with birthing their babies, getting them to urgent and specialist care as needed, supporting them through the tough times, sharing in the joys and the pains. There was so much in my work that I enjoyed.

However, from the first months in practice, I met patients that came to me with conditions that I could not diagnose or had questions that I could not answer. I began to experience the burden of patient's demands to know what was wrong with them, wanting to be told what to do, and asking for a pill to make them better. More and more I felt I was skimming the surface of things, giving out band-aid solutions, not knowing and not being able to deal with the cause. I was left feeling frustrated and ineffective.

I thought perhaps I didn't know enough, so I took more courses which gave me more knowledge of how to treat and manage disease, but it still didn't help me answer many of my patients' questions of why they were getting sick and how they could get better.

As close as I felt to being in a career of my choice, I was not happy. I began to feel more and more insignificant in my ability to make a difference to the health of my patients, especially those with cancer, who despite maximum therapy and even good results, returned to me in fear for their lives. I felt powerless to help.

I considered quitting. However, I also sensed that I was in no emotional state to make such a decision. To find relief from my feelings of distress, I took a holiday, returned somewhat restored, and managed to shift my outlook enough to make the decision to just accept that I was unhappy with my work, put all my troubles "on the back burner" as it were, and focus on anything that made me feel good.

I remember it was summer and I focused on playing and relaxing – picnic lunches, a bike ride, or walk after work with a friend. Within a couple of weeks I noticed I was smiling more and even making jokes at work. "Oh, that's interesting." Where did I learn that play and fun couldn't be a part of work? Ah… I had perceived that work was serious business by watching my Dad. I said to myself, "That style doesn't work for me."

I had lightened up enough to then ask myself, "What do I like about my work?" I liked counseling my patients in ways that they could help themselves. I liked giving information about health promotion and disease prevention. And then a single word floated into my awareness, coming up from the depths of my being, and that word was "healing."

Recognizing that one word, a rush of aliveness and tingling came over me. That's it! That's what I want to be about. In the same moment I realized that I had never heard the word "healing" once in all my medical training, or ever in conversations with medical colleagues. I'd heard "cure," "best outcome," but never "healing." And I knew nothing about healing. All I could say was that it had to involve the emotions.

I might have become frustrated with my not knowing, but instead I allowed myself to not know and I asked for help. I very simply put out to the Universe, "Show me the small steps to healing for myself, and that I might show them to others." It became my mantra that I would send out almost every day, and I waited.

Very soon Life began bringing me experiences for which no book or training had prepared me. I went through an intense few months when three of my patients were diagnosed with cancer. One was a young woman in her thirties and she was dying. I said to myself, "I don't know if I can handle this. I'm not prepared for this." So I took a week-long course in palliative care which gave me more medical skills and confidence. My patient turned out to be my teacher instead. She showed so much courage and strength, and there was so much love between her and her husband that embraced her and everyone around her. Once I had done all I could medically, I learned to let go of controlling the outcome. That was between my patient and her "God." In sitting with her, not having any textbook to tell me how, I discovered a place in me where I didn't have to do anything - where I could simply be present and compassionate, holding a space of rest, of loving regard, for my patient and myself.

It wasn't until later that I received the full awareness of the gifts my patient had given me – to get out of fear in facing cancer in others and my own sense of helplessness, and to recognize that my quality of presence with my patient was healing in and of itself.

I kept learning about healing and listening to the promptings of an inner voice. I learned that I didn't have to have all the answers. I learned that we each hold the answers we need. I learned that my job could be one of guiding my patients to move past their fears, towards empowerment to become their own healers.

I can now say to anyone who tells me they have hit the wall, "Good! It is better than dropping off the cliff." When we hit the wall and feel most stuck, we are getting ready for the breakthrough to great revelation and growth.

If I were to give a prescription for dealing with feeling lost or stuck in your life, it would include the following:

1. In the first instance, accept where you are, rather than push against the wall and reinforce what you don't want in your life.

2. Take a holiday from the mind's effort to find a solution. Breathe deep – it will relax you and take you out of your mind and all the spinning thoughts. Do whatever you can to bring lightness and joy, pleasure and fun into your experience. Walk in nature, soak in a bubble bath, dance, or sing in the shower. Whatever brings you into your body will bring you out of your mind, closer to your heart, and into the present moment.

3. Take time to be quiet with yourself so you can hear your inner voice. Meditation or a yoga practice helps.

4. When you feel ready, start an inquiry –

   • What do I value? What do I really care about?

   • How do I want to feel, and what makes me feel that way?

   • What do I really enjoy and have fun doing?

   • What am I here in this Life for? What is my gift?

I have often used the following steps to help someone who feels lost.

Step 1 - Write down everything that you have ever enjoyed or appreciated in your life at any time - activities, experiences, talents that you have, qualities that you like about yourself. Brainstorm, or as I prefer to say "heart-storm" it, and have fun with it. Let everything come up from as far back in childhood as you want. Don't censor anything or make any judgment. Be curious. Let it be a celebration of you.

Step 2 - Write down three things you think would make the world a better place. Take your time to quietly and easily reflect on this. Don't force anything. Your answer is your deepest truth and will often just float to the surface when you least expect it, as my word "healing" did for me.

Step 3 - Finally, look for the contributions in Step 1 that support your answers in Step 2. This match will clarify what you really care about and give you some direction.

Keep moving towards what you believe in and care about and celebrate yourself for the small steps you make along the way. Remember to keep nurturing and loving yourself. Remember to enjoy the journey. Keep doing what you feel inspired to do, what enlivens you; what makes your heart sing.

Whatever path is taken, the direction is the same – to follow the calling of the heart to bring your gift into the world for yourself and all around you.

Dr. Nelie Johnson is a practicing family physician in British Columbia, Canada. From her awareness that Medicine was unable to respond to all the needs of her patients, she undertook extensive studies in breakthrough knowledge about healing. She shares this knowledge through seminars, workshops and private consultations that provide tools that open her patients to the possibility of fully healing themselves. For more information and free information, visit www.AwarenessHeals.ca.

Remember to Stop and Just Breathe

~⌒⌒

Colleen Bain, M.A

Life is filled with experiences—some small and some grand—which affect us in some way.

For me, one such experience was in 1998. My eleven-month-old daughter, Shannon, was diagnosed with Opscolonus Myoclonus Syndrome (OMS) - a rare autoimmune disorder that impacts 1 in 10 million children a year, causes brain injury, and is usually accompanied with neuroblastoma (cancerous tumor).

When the doctors announced the cancer to me, I immediately asked if she was going to die. The doctors replied they just didn't know. More testing was needed. I was alone when they delivered this news, as my husband had just stepped out of the room. This sent me on an emotional roller coaster as I tried to fathom that my baby daughter might not be with me in just seven days. I also had to tell my husband that his baby girl had cancer and might not live. I felt as if my soul was holding on by a thread trying to remain in my body. As I stood there in the cold, dank hospital room, I held Shannon, dressed in her pink coordinated dress, bow, and shoes, tightly to my chest. As she looked up at me and smiled, I felt very alone and overwhelmed. In that instant, I felt the huge responsibility of saving Shannon's life resting on my shoulders. When I looked back down into her bluish green eyes, tears began streaming down my face, sprinkling onto her little body. There were too many thoughts spiraling out of control in my mind. I needed to do something quickly.

I took a few deep breaths, wiped my tears off my cheeks, and stiffened my spine. I firmly stated to the doctors that I was not going to inform my husband that his baby girl had cancer and OMS — let alone that she might die. I demanded the doctors take charge of delivering this message immediately upon my husband's return to the room. When he returned I watched helplessly as my husband fell to his knees and cried in despair. There was little we could do. Shannon's destiny was in God's hands. The years that followed that dreary day were to be the most difficult ones of my life. Shannon did live and survived the cancer; however, the OMS turned out to be a monster. Exhaustion and sadness were to become my constant companions.

The OMS caused havoc on Shannon's central nervous system. She was unable to tell the difference between her feet and her head, relative to the space around her, and this was only one of the many symptoms of OMS. As a result, Shannon attached herself to me to confirm her safety. Rarely was I ever separated from her. She was in constant fear of falling, even when upright. Now my one-year-old baby was having daily rage attacks for over two hours at a clip, kicking, biting, screaming, and punching me until her little body finally gave up and left us both exhausted. Every night for almost six years, my husband walked Shannon in her carriage for hours to help her get some sleep. Just about every day, I drove Shannon for hours so she could sleep.

Every day I had to inject my baby with life threatening drugs to save her life. How ironic, as these injections were one of many situations that put her life in jeopardy. For example, when Shannon was about fifteen months old, she went through plasmapheresis, which removes antibodies from the blood. During one of the sessions, her port had ruptured and broken. Blood was shooting from her chest towards the ceiling of the hospital room. Shannon was screaming for me. I knew if she saw me she would want me to hold her and tell her everything was going to be fine. However, I could not do that because her blood was leaving her so fast there was no time for hugs and kisses. I stayed in the room, but out of Shannon's reach. All I wanted to do was pick up my baby, kiss her, and take the pain away. Frozen in fear, I just paced back and forth saying, "God, please help my baby girl." I had to keep reminding myself to just breathe. Ten minutes later, a surgeon came in to help the frantic nurses. He placed a clamp on Shannon's vein and removed the bloodied towels from her chest. Shannon survived.

Three years after her initial diagnosis, Shannon was off her medications. I had to learn how to manage the residual waxing and waning of recurring symptoms triggered by stress and infections. She was sick most days after starting school. The days she did make it to school were filled with frustration. Her brain injury weakened her ability to learn. At the end of Kindergarten, I agreed to hold Shannon back, a decision I would later regret. I did not realize this at the time, but without strong cognitive skills, repeating the learning was useless.

By the time Shannon was ten, I knew there had to be a better way. Either I was going to shrivel up and become just another victim of life, or I was going to once again wipe the tears from my face, take a deep breath, and stand up tall.

I told God that I was not going to live my life or let Shannon live like this anymore. I wasn't going to settle for overcoming the situation; I intended to become a champion. I did not know how this was going to happen, but I passionately believed that with faith there was hope.

Once I made this decision, my life began to change. Ideas and resources began showing up. One thought that kept appearing in my mind was cognitive rehabilitation. Usually after a person receives a traumatic brain injury, he/she is given cognitive rehabilitation, along with speech, occupational, and physical therapy. Shannon received years of the latter, but not once did she get cognitive rehabilitation.

The next step was taking action on my thoughts and ideas. I began researching cognitive strengthening programs that would work for Shannon and other children with OMS. Shortly thereafter I was led to a research-based brain training program and, after six months of researching the program, I became certified as a provider and trainer. I trained Shannon's brain for three months. Before the brain training, Shannon was seen as learning challenged. After the brain training program, she began to learn again.

In fact, she was just accepted in a prominent private school. Although she has a long road ahead of her, she continues her journey of being a champion of OMS. She's also beginning a new journey of self-discovery to allow her life purpose to grow wings and take flight.

I believe everyone who reads my story can become a champion of his or her own life circumstances. You see, life is not simply good or bad, but rather one learning experience after another. When you have a *bad* experience, intend to overcome it. Next, be aware of people, thoughts, or resources that come your way. Take action on those aligned with your intentions. As you follow this process, you will recognize that your experiences become easier to *manage* and *champion* as you continue your journey. Remember, life is meant to be fun, creative, and uplifting.

I believe you are meant to discover your life purpose through the many situations you overcome. As you live your life's purpose, you help others discover their passion.

For me, once I saw the positive impact brain training had on my daughter, I created a business that gives students the ability to learn, while helping them become champions in academic areas that were once a struggle. By doing this, my students have a chance to discover their life's passion. They feel fulfilled and inspired to help others discover their life's joy.

Along my journey to becoming a champion of OMS and my life, I learned a few strategies that continue to inspire and empower me and those around me. First, remember to connect with God - your creator, the main source of your life. Knowing you are one with your Creator is powerful. Secondly, keep focused on the one thing that is in front of you. Do not allow your thoughts to wander to the past or future. Avoid worry and enjoy the gift of now. Thirdly, keep your mindset as positive as possible. By slowing down and focusing on good thoughts, you will have more clarity and ease of decision making. Fourth, do not lose sight of being connected with a support group. Being connected with others who have overcome the situation you are presently enduring is extremely helpful. Lastly, but most importantly, remember to stop and just breathe. Breathing fills your heart with God's love. God's love will bring light to your dark situation. Your situation will become more manageable and you will overcome it.

"Learning is experiencing. Everything else is just information."

- ALBERT EINSTEIN

Colleen Bain *has a master's degree in special education and is a licensed special and general educator in the state of New Jersey. As a licensed brain trainer, she transforms students from struggling learners to exhilarated individuals with an enhanced ability to learn easily and efficiently in record time. Stop by Colleen's website, www.els4kids.com, today and get your copy of her Free report, 5* Steps to Improve a Child's Academic Success in Reading and Math.

The Call to Trust and Believe in Healing Love

Lalei Gutierrez

Returning to the Setting

In 2003 I found myself on a plane heading back to a country I'd left behind twenty-seven years earlier during a time of terror. Now I was returning to the Philippines for a joyous event, my daughter's wedding

To attend this special event in my daughter's life, I had to return to the scene of my most difficult life choice, a life or death decision. I chose life.

A. Flashback: Beginnings of the Journey

I was in my early thirties when the world I knew came crashing down. Martial law was declared in my home country. Friends and colleagues were missing or taken political prisoners, and fear gripped many. Chaos and instability shook all levels of society.

Together with my professional group of applied behavioral scientists, I was an impassioned activist, facilitating human relations and leadership training groups to raise consciousness and foster integrity, human dignity, and freedom. I worked tirelessly for an end to injustice. The mounting dissonance between my values and the circumstances of life became unbearable. Pressure from powerful forces ripped apart my marriage. Political corruption, shame, and infidelity became the "elephants" in my home. Truth shook my soul. Freedom to face the truth versus the oppression of going along played its painful hand.

Fighting desperately against the downward grip of depression, I cried vehemently to God. "Is this my life? I am dying inside! So much anger, apathy, dishonesty, greed...so much poverty! Is this the world for my children? My daughter is a beautiful soul. Will you let the daughters of the world be imprisoned by fear and exploitation? Do something! Spare my children from this legacy! It is unfair, God. Where are You? Where are our human rights? I must release this pain!"

I prayed for miracles. Then, one night I was awakened from a dream. Radiant light filled my room. My name was called. I heard a calm voice vibrate in the stillness of silence, *"Your prayers are answered. Trust and believe. Someone will approach you with directions. Pay attention. Follow and tell nobody."* Amazing peace embraced my whole being.

B. Dilemma and Choice

With such a risk to heed the compelling call, a dialogue with The Voice made one thing very clear: I must entrust my children into God's loving protection and leave them behind.

The Voice spoke, "You will be judged as irresponsible, shameful, and scandalous by standards of this world here. This security is a fleeting illusion. Have courage as I am with you."

While my prayers were being answered, I risked leaping with faith to live the questions with trust and belief, and to be open to pay attention to the unfolding answers. I was willing to do whatever The Voice asked me to do, even though I did not know what would follow.

C. The Calling

Then, I was called. What a huge CALL this was! One that had no words. One that asked me to fight for my life and for my children by leaving them first. I was being called to leave my county, my family, my profession, my culture, and everything familiar. Even more challenging, I was being called to do this in silence, with no goodbyes or closure.

D. Encounter with Obstacles

Even though travel was banned, I was called to escort thirty-three diverse emigrants to Canada. I had no idea how to do this task, nor time to do anything but trust and obey. I was to leave immediately.

The journey was full of perils and miracles. At every turn, help was provided at just the right time, often from mysterious sources. When the group of emigrants was safely delivered to new homes in Canada, I was called next to the United States, where I knew no one.

I arrived with meager money, no place to live and an invitation to attend a professional training seminar at a university. However, I was never alone. The Inner Voice's presence guided helpful, positive people to align in fulfilling the Higher Purpose of my journey. Prayer became my constant companion.

Process of Overcoming: Guided by Spirit

My heart ached for my children. No logic, training, or religion prepared me for the descent into the void of pain and longing I experienced. To live *one day at a time* was the only way I could manage the tidal waves of choking grief. The losses and loneliness of my inner landscape were momentarily interrupted by the *amazing beauty of nature's seasons* and *people's kindness* upon my arrival in a foreign land. Somehow, I survived.

Most importantly, in my daily meditations on the Miracles of Love, I visualized myself with my children, playing, singing, reading, hugging, laughing, and loving each other as we used to do. I saw them in my mind, fully alive, free, and thriving. I tapped into an energetic realm wherein connecting with my children's beingness moved me with awe and respect for their souls' journey. I discovered I could still love and support them energetically, even if I could not do so in the physical realm.

Spiritually guided, I was brought to postgraduate clinical training, which opened doors to supportive friends and colleagues, allowing me to obtain a doctorate in psychology. I went on to establish a practice as an integrative psychologist, couples systems and diversity consultant, energy healing practitioner, and holistic life, relations, and spiritual coach.

My journey to inner freedom meant facing the shadows of early childhood, cultural oppressions, and traumatic decisions to fight for aliveness. Profound shifts occurred. Manure turned into fertilizer, transforming experiences of the past to a present of well-being, compassion, forgiveness, empowerment, creativity, inspiration, gratitude, and wisdom.

A recurring dream of a spiritually loving partnership was a cherished secret for many years. Then, one beautiful day in the fall of 1984, while designing a workshop with my dear friend and colleague, Phil, a radiant light lifted the veil from my eyes. All fear left my bones. I felt overwhelmed with the Gift of Love that Spirit had waited for me to embrace. This was the man who would be my partner in life and in love.

Our conscious healing partnership laid the safe haven for the process of our children's establishing their US home here with us. We discovered ways to form an international family connection that led to a physical reunion. To be able to hug my children again, to mother them, to love them in person as well as in spirit, was a miracle. Our healing partnership expanded to bring many more healing love transformations to the people Spirit sends us to serve.

Full Circle

My daughter's wedding allowed me the opportunity to revisit my culture of origin. While I could have been fearful to return to the Philippines, I was held in Radiant Light, knowing that the Holy Spirit is larger than all the happenings that take place. Grace and blessings overshadowed any old sadnesses and grief. I could return to the Philippines happy, whole, and healed.

Within another four years, our two sons married. Each one brought their own depth of meaning to their love relationships. Each one saw their life journey and growth to be beyond their weddings. Each one grappled with generational messages culture passed on, to go to the heart of LOVE and make courageous and conscious choices of the Spirit.

Profoundly touched by my children's expressions of heartfelt gratitude and encouragement to write the stories of my life and life lessons learned, I am grateful for the spiritual gift of their presence in my life. Their amazing love has impelled and inspired me to participate in co-creating a loving, peaceful, and kinder world.

What I Learned

The Inner Voice is my constant guidepost of God's embodied presence within me. When I become too busy, restlessness is my body's signal to listen within. As I breathe and slow down, the stillness of my sacred space attunes to allow Love's radiance to be an inspiring healing presence in navigating the pathways of my life and work.

My life journey has been one of healing love, turning life's "manure" into fertilizer for learning, growth, and wisdom. I learned to trust and believe that the greatest force and tool we have to heal our world is love. In reclaiming our loving Inner Self, we participate in healing the world together. Experiences, especially ones that are the hardest, have gold to be found by sifting through the dirt and pain to find the miracles of Love waiting for you there.

Lalei E. Gutierrez Ph.D., LSMFT, RPE, CPC, *is a holistic psychologist, life, relationship and spiritual coach, couples system and diversity consultant. Her practice reflects her love and gratitude to serve, with a Higher Purpose, individuals, couples, families, groups and the world community through their life journeys, transitions, aspirations, transformative process and well-being. To learn of her collaborative body-emotion-energy-mind-spirit process and practice (BEEMS) method, check www.PhilLalei.com, and their e-book for Healing Love relationships at www.TenPathwaysofHealingLove.com.*

How the Airline Safety Speech Saved My Life

Amelie Chance

The plane taxied down the runway as we watched a flight attendant mime the FAA safety instructions in perfect timing to the recorded message overhead. "Should oxygen be needed, a mask will drop down from the compartment located above your seats…" I had traveled so extensively that these words generally glossed over me, but this time was different. This time I heard a distinct and powerful message, so I turned to my husband and said, "Kal, I want a divorce."

The blood drained from his face. After several long moments he responded, "We never fight, I treat you well, and our careers…they're thriving. I don't understand what it is that you want."

"I want love," I replied simply.

"Amelie, we've only been married for six months. We can make this work. Anyway, we don't get divorced," he said with a now discernible edge in his voice.

The "we" he was referring to were Indians. You see, Kal was short for Kalpesh, and though my parents had oddly given me a French name, we were both 100% Indian American. Like our first generation peers, we identified strongly with both our culture from India and from America, and with respect to marriage, most of us erred on the Indian side. I believe, "Just make it work," was the unwritten rule. Kal was also correct that we had wed only 6 months earlier and had I the strength to know myself sooner, we wouldn't be in this predicament. I placed a protective hand on my forehead, preparing for the memory I knew this conversation would conjure.

I was in the hallway calming my nerves with long, deep breaths before I cracked the door open to confirm the rumors. It was true, my mom had outdone herself - the décor was exquisite. The room dripped endlessly with gossamer bows and red flora. Roses, matured to perfection, enveloped each support column, creating an illusion of giant floral trees soaring towards the sky. The satin-draped chairs were set in a precise semi-circle, parting only once to highlight an aisle adorned with shimmering crystal vases and ending in a striking mandap, the traditional Indian wedding canopy. It seemed everything in the room was alive. That is, everything except for me. This was the worst day in all of my twenty-four years. It was my wedding day.

The music began and my heart leapt into a sprint, urging my legs to follow. I stood in my ornate Indian lengha, a two- piece outfit with a blouse and long skirt weighing over fifty pounds, covered in small roses crafted from real gold thread and held up by a pair of hidden suspenders. Various escape routes traced my thoughts, yet more than the weight of my dress, the load of my indecision held me motionless. I watched as my oversized bridal party flowed into that purposefully slow progression down the aisle, leaving me in temporary isolation.

I closed my eyes, hoping for a moment of peace; instead I was struck by the roar of my mind. "Amelie, there is still time. Turn around - run away!" It was my intuition that prior to that day had only offered broken whispers, but the voice did not speak unopposed. As always, my false logic provided an alternative, "No, Amelie, this is the right person. Look at the bliss that has spread around you." Suddenly my internal quarrel drowned into the music, the wedding march had begun. It was too late. So, I kicked my brocade gown one careful step in front of another and walked directly into the biggest mistake of my life.

The plane jarred from turbulence, springing me back to reality. Kal was tugging my arm while insisting, "It's only been six months, let's try."

I just shook my head and he whispered, "I cannot believe this – we are perfect for each other."

Perfect for each other he had thought. I don't blame him, it's what I thought until deep into our engagement, when it became clear the perfection was only on paper –good careers, the same culture, and a handsome couple. It was more like a corporate merger than a relationship success. In fact, when we were in one another's company, it was…well, BLAH. Maybe if we were two inherently boring individuals that came together to create an even more uninspired couple, I could possibly accept the status quo. Yet standing alone, I had a boisterous personality interested in politics, psychology, business, and friendships and he could speak endlessly about medicine and track and field. It's not so much that our interests diverged; it's that there was not a single intersection. Moreover, we lacked basic chemistry – sexual and conversational.

The truth was that I never laughed less than when I was with Kal, and a void inside of me started to grow, rapidly and unhindered. I felt as if a rogue force was squashing pieces of my personality until I finally defended the pain with silence. I would go to work, come home, and try to sleep as early as possible. He filled these gaps with television and medical journals, but I knew it was only a matter of time before the state of our relationship encroached on his happiness as well.

I finally responded, "Kal, we're totally *imperfect* for each other. If it were a palpable problem, like abuse or infidelity, maybe we'd have a chance with therapy, but our issue is far worse. Our issue is indifference."

"But that's not true, I care about…well, I care about you," he said and then hesitantly asked, "Why did you agree to marry me?"

I thought about it and the answer was utterly lucid - I put the happiness of others ahead of my own. Everyone was so thrilled at this union. There weren't any frogs lined up at my door waiting to be turned into princes, and he seemed to fit a mold I'd been presented with early in life. It seemed good enough, so I settled and frankly, so had he.

As forthright as possible, I answered, "I thought I could float on the happiness of those around me. I now see that it just doesn't work that way."

He shook his head again and asked almost to himself, "Do you understand what it's going to be like for *us* to get divorced?"

Of course I had thought about it. I was plagued by the awful semantics. The sentence, "We would be the first in our families…" is usually followed by, "to go to college" or something cheerful. For us it would be, "to get divorced." Everyone makes mistakes in their life; the difference is that most are afforded the opportunity to overcome these mistakes privately. I knew divorce was not as such in our case – it was a public blunder. I feared the unveiled judgments from extended family and how that would affect our parents. I loathed the concept of dividing up furniture and friendships. I cringed at society's obsession with marital status. Did the dentist really need to know if I were single, married, divorced, or widowed before filling a cavity? But all of my anxieties, all my trepidations combined were dwarfed by one greater fear: denying myself the chance to be happy.

I responded only with the truth I had heard earlier. "Kal, the flight attendant instructed us to place an oxygen mask securely on our *own* face before offering assistance to others. This concept was never intuitive to me, but I now understand. It is a basic survival skill, a prerequisite for happiness. Before extending happiness beyond my own person,

I must first offer it to myself."

Breaking up was not easy, but the worst periods were suffered in anticipation, rather than the actual moments. I dreaded delivering the news to my parents, yet after quietly listening to my story, they offered their full support and even expressed pride in my decision. My father explained I would always have their blessing if it meant opening the door to a happier life. My additional fear of being a divorcee branded with a scarlet letter of sorts dissolved when several friends said I had inspired them to make difficult decisions in their own lives.

An experience like divorce becomes a vital part of one's history, lending strength to character and encouraging new endeavors. In my case, it has helped me expand and sell my business, move to New York, re-enter the dating scene, find the companionship of a genuine soul mate, and discover a career assisting others with recovery from a broken heart. I believe for each of us to unearth our authentic path, we must step out of the world sculpted by the expectations of others and into one supporting our genuine desires. In this, we are not only rewarded for our courage, but that courage often takes on a momentum that helps fulfill our every dream.

Amelie Chance has a BA in Finance. She began her career as a financial consultant, after which she ran a mid-size technology company. Amelie later abandoned her left-brained profession to pursue her passion for writing. Her niche includes providing relationship advice based on techniques of positive psychology. Download a Free copy of Amelie & Als' 10 Step Process to Recovery From a Broken Heart, including 3 bonus steps available only at www.HealMyBrokenHeart.com/overcomers.

When Your Intuition Calls, Answer the Phone!

Rev. Rita "MeKila" Herring

Shortly after being laid off work in 1992, I began receiving messages that I needed to go to Germany. My mother was born and grew up in Germany, and had met my father there while he was in the military. They married and moved to the United States, but all of my mother's relatives still lived in Germany.

The first nudging I received was a very strong feeling that I needed to go there. It had been nineteen years since I'd visited, yet it seemed to be such a poor time to even consider it. I've always listened to my intuition, but this time, due to the timing, I questioned its viability. In my daily prayer time I asked for further guidance. "If this is truly something that I need to do, please give me blatantly obvious messages that I can't possibly misinterpret."

The very next day at church, one of my fellow ministers came up to me, placed her hands on my shoulders, looked into my eyes and said, *"You need to go to Germany!"* I asked her why she would say that. She and I had been watching the fares to Germany for several years as she, like my mom, is originally from there. The fares had always been out of our reach. "A round trip flight to Germany right now is only $464!" is what she said. I thought, "My, that's pretty clear now, isn't it?" My mind was reeling. How was I going to pull this off? I had little income and had been living paycheck to paycheck, so I had no savings.

That afternoon my boyfriend of the time was taking a shower and singing the song, "Playground in My Mind." When he got to the part that says, *"I'm gonna' let them visit their grandma ..."* he turned off the water, grabbed his checkbook, and **wrote a check for the airfare.** My grandmother was still alive and perhaps *that* was the reason for my messages.

One of my favorite spiritual guides has always been my Opa (Grandfather in German). He died on my ninth birthday and yet I felt closer to him after his death than before, as I had only met him once in real life. I got the distinct impression that he was instrumental in my feelings of needing to go there. I said, "Opa, if you REALLY think that I need to go, please show me a sign that this is something that I should pursue."

Now that the airfare was in my hands, I began to wonder about my passport. I hadn't seen it in years and wondered if it was still valid. I had several boxes in the garage of things I hadn't gone through since moving to California - perhaps it was there. That afternoon as I opened the drawer to my file cabinet (which I used daily) something fell out and hit me on the foot. **It was my passport!** It was expired so I called the passport agency to see what the procedure was for renewal. I was advised NOT to go to a satellite office, but to come to the main office in San Francisco, as it would take two weeks to process the renewal.

On Tuesday afternoon, I hopped onto BART (Bay Area Rapid Transit) and arrived at the Passport office a few moments before they were to close. I chatted with the gentleman that was processing my renewal and asked if it would really take two weeks. He said he would see what he could do to expedite the process.

That Thursday I went to the mailbox and in it was **my renewed passport!** I immediately booked my flight. I was to fly into Frankfurt, which was much farther north than my relatives, who live in the Munich area. This was of no concern to me, as my minister friend would be meeting me and we'd take it from there.

My mother was surprisingly non-supportive. I couldn't figure this out, as she had always been an encouraging force in my life. Still, after four strong indicators to go, I was now determined. I called her from Canada as I was changing planes. "Mom, can I PLEASE have *anyone's* phone number?" "Oh honey, just go have a good time. You don't have to see our relatives this time. There's a thunderstorm here right now and I can't see the phone book. You'll have other chances to see them. Your grandmother is no longer in her house. She fell, broke her hip, and is living in a rehabilitation/retirement home, so you will not be able to find her." This was the first I'd heard about that and I wondered if that was somehow the reason for this adventure.

As I did not speak German, I was really heading blindly into this endeavor. At first my minister friend helped me by being my translator. Soon this became too much for her and while we were sitting in the Frankfort Magistrate's office, attempting to locate a particular relative, she threw up her arms and said, "I can't do this anymore! German-English, English-German!" With that she stormed off, leaving me with the Magistrate official. We just smiled at one another and I took off in the opposite direction. When I was alone, I sat down and began to speak with my Opa. "Opa, this was YOUR idea! YOU wanted me to come here! Now I need some HELP!"

I began to digest German at an amazing rate. Each day I became more fluent. I began to travel down the center of Germany. When I arrived at my mother's hometown of Augsburg, I looked in the phone book and found her brother. I reached my aunt, asked her where my grandmother was, and she gave me the name of the home my grandmother was in. I had just enough time to find what buses I needed to take and to get there before visiting hours were over.

The hotel manager assisted me and I was on my way. After changing buses several times, I was now only a couple of blocks from where my grandmother was. I ran the rest of the way. Upon arrival I found her name and room number on the board and hurried to see her. As I reached her room, I discovered that she shared it with a completely non-responsive lady in a wheelchair whose head was always bent forward. The room was amazingly hot as this little lady was quite frail and needed it to be so. My grandmother, as bright and alert as ever, was surprised to see me. We chatted for a short while before it was time for me to go.

As I rode the buses back to the hotel, I pondered her situation. She shared a room with that other lady, with only a small table and chair which it turns out she never used. She had a bed and a small armoire with a few articles of clothing. Her personal effects included only a crucifix and a picture of her wedding day. She was 95 years old and spent her days sitting on the edge of her bed. My heart was breaking.

The next day while visiting, we walked arm-in-arm down the hallways. I asked her why she didn't have an Einzelzimmer, (single room). She said, *"Wenn mann zufrieden ist, kan mann immer glücklich sein,"* which means, "When one is content, one is always happy." Oh well, that's nice, but it was *not* satisfactory to me. Each time we'd pass a single room, I'd slow down, look in and say in German, "Look Oma, how nice." She'd look for a moment and then pull me forward.

I did some digging around and found out that no one pursued the single room option because my grandmother said she was fine with her current living accommodations. Well, guess what? It wasn't fine with me! I called my mom, told her of the situation, and got her on the job, as this was also unacceptable to her. I was only able to stay a short time, so nothing transpired while I was there, but within a month of my return home she had a single room – just in time for Christmas.

She was now able to have more of her personal possessions, and could sleep with the windows open – something she'd done her whole life. She was able to have a small Christmas tree. My relatives said she just blossomed. She lived to be one hundred and one and I am so very grateful that I listened to my intuition and followed my inner nudgings.

In this day and age it's so very important that we listen to our intuition, and it's really not that hard to do. The more you practice listening, the more clearly the messages come. The more you trust your "gut feeling," the more you develop that intuitive muscle. Listen to your inner voice. Know that my love and support are ever with you.

MeKila has been an ordained minister since 1986 and a certified clinical hypnotherapist since 1992. It's always been her desire to assist others in realizing their empowerment. She's an insatiable student of human-ness, experiencer of miracles, believer of oneness and lover of life. She lives on Kauai, Hawaii, with her best friends: her hubby, David, and spry seventeen year-old puppy, Lani. For a Free report on intuition, visit her website www.MeKila.com.

The Waiting Room Miracle

Lynne Klippel

"We're ready to take him now." The nurse started to wheel the stretcher with my six-year-old son towards the doors of the surgery department. I tried hard not to let Jacob see my tears or my fears.

Jacob, the youngest of my three sons, had an egg-sized tumor on his shin bone. After visiting several physicians, we were at the regional children's hospital where a surgeon would remove the tumor and determine if it was cancerous.

I was a wreck, worried about my son not being able to run or play, or worse, having cancer. As I sat in the waiting room chair, a new worry crossed my mind. I'd have to spend the next stressful hours sitting in that room with my ex-husband, Bob.

We'd divorced after a ten-year marriage in which Bob fought a losing battle with mental illness. As he became more ill, it seemed too dangerous to live with him, so I left abruptly with the boys. Six years later, Bob was more stable, but our relationship was still very strained. We argued frequently and avoided each other so that things would appear calm to our children.

Now we were sitting in the same room in a very stressful situation. I was frightened and began to pray. I asked God to protect Jacob and heal him. Then I asked God to protect me, to make sure that everyone stayed calm, and that no arguments would break out while we were in the hospital.

I prayed for a long time. While I was praying, a sudden peace came over me. It seemed like I could sense the arms of God holding me. The word forgiveness flashed into my mind.

Was I supposed to forgive Bob for all the things he'd done to me during our marriage and afterwards?

My first thought was, "No way!" Terrible things happened during our marriage; frightening, hurtful, deeply scarring things. I wore the scars like a badge of courage, proud to have had the gumption to leave and build a new life for myself and my children. I told other women my story about walking away from my pretty house and good job to a small apartment and food stamps. I joked about selling plasma to pay the light bill, even though just the telling of this terrible time made me feel ashamed deep down.

Over six years, I'd used my fear and anger as fuel to rebuild my life. Things were good now. I had a new career, enough money to pay the bills, and the boys were doing well. I'd even been blessed with a new, happy marriage. People who knew my story seemed inspired by it and told me I was brave and strong.

Honestly, I did not think I could ever forgive Bob for the things that happened during our marriage. Who would I be if I gave up my victim story and forgave him?

Then, a new thought burst into my mind: could I forgive myself as well?

I felt a terrible sense of guilt about the failure of my marriage. Although I knew logically that I had to leave, I knew I'd made mistakes too. I replayed scenes from our marriage in my mind like a movie, seeing many times where I should have done something differently.

I'd always wanted to be a wife and a mother. I was smart, worked very hard, and tried to live my life according to my spiritual beliefs, yet my marriage had been a nightmare instead of the fairy tale life I had imagined as a young girl. How did I allow divorce to happen to me?

Sitting silently in that hospital waiting room, I was confronted by some ugly truths. My life looked great on the outside, but internally I was full of anger, bitterness, and guilt. My busy lifestyle had kept me from paying attention to those dark feelings, and I covered them up with a big smile and lots of activity.

Bob was not my enemy. I wasn't the perfectly innocent victim. We both shared responsibility for the demise of our marriage.

I started to argue with God in my head. It seemed like He'd brought the two of us together, stuck for hours in the waiting room, so that forgiveness and healing could occur. Didn't He know that I was worried sick about my little boy? Why this? And better yet, why now?

It took a lot of courage, but I had a good conversation with Bob that day. We talked for a long time about our marriage and how much we both loved our sons. We apologized to each other and offered forgiveness in return. It seemed like a miracle that we could have a civil conversation after so many years of angry arguments and accusations. Some of the bitterness started to dissolve. I felt peace enter my heart as I forgave him and started to forgive myself.

Just after our conversation wound to a close, the doctor entered the waiting room. Jacob was fine! The tumor was benign and much easier to remove than anyone anticipated. Jacob was out of surgery in a couple of hours instead of the six to eight hours we anticipated. This was the second miracle of the day and we all rejoiced!

This story took place eight years ago. Today Jacob is a healthy, active teen. He has a large scar on his leg, but no other side effects of his surgery.

Bob and I now have a cordial relationship. When he had a car accident, I picked him up from the hospital. When my parents became ill, he offered support and took care of the boys. We still don't see eye-to-eye on many things, but we can sit beside each other without feelings of repressed anger, and watch Jacob play football and cheer him on enthusiastically. We can talk about our sons and marvel at their growth. Somehow we've found common ground.

Most importantly, I've forgiven myself over the failure of my first marriage. Guilt and shame no longer haunt me. Letting go of my anger and victim story was the first step to a deep emotional healing for me.

This experience taught me that it is possible to forgive someone who has deeply hurt you. I'll never condone some of the things Bob did to me during our marriage, but I do forgive him for doing them. Even the bitterest of enemies can forge a positive relationship if God can open their hearts to forgiveness.

Forgiveness is freeing. Once I was able to let go of the anger and pain of my past, I experienced a joy and peace that I never expected. When I stopped focusing on my victim story, I was healed and able to move forward with my life. This was my miracle.

What about you?

Do you carry around a load of bitterness, guilt, and shame left over from your past? What if you could forgive yourself and the one who hurt you, so that you could be free?

If you are in need of forgiveness, be gentle with yourself. Get the support of a trusted friend, therapist, or spiritual mentor who can encourage and support you through the process. Pray. Find the courage to take one last look at the darkness of your past and then release it.

When you do, you will walk into the sunshine of today, reborn and renewed. You will be healed and whole. You will be free.

Lynne Klippel *is an author, coach, and publisher. She helps entrepreneurs write books to build their business and share their knowledge. If you have a book inside you, Lynne's audio,* Write Your Book the RIGHT Way," *can help you unleash the hidden words within your heart. Visit www.LoveYourLifePublishing.com and download your free copy today.*

Willy Loman,
I Am Not!

Kimberly L. Martin

In my view, selling is a sleazy, un-respected, tragic profession, and the antithesis of healthcare work! That's exactly what I believed to be true when I was working as an Athletic Therapist in the late 1980's. I was assessing and rehabilitating athletes with musculo-skeletal injuries, on the field and in the clinic. So, how did I become a top-selling, award-winning corporate sales rep?

One of my first jobs after graduation was running a rehab clinic. This included set up of the treatment area, bringing in and treating clients. During the purchase of treatment modalities, I was visited by the company rep that sold me the equipment I needed. In one of our meetings he mentioned they were looking to hire a new sales rep, and he thought I would be a good fit for the job. I said, "No way! I read *Death of a Salesman* and I am not going to be Willy Loman!"

The convincing moment came when he told me that the position paid *double* what I was currently making. I was young and money was scarce, so it seemed like a good idea at the time. But guess what? I was a horrible sales person! I found it excruciatingly difficult to "sell" to other healthcare professionals. I felt so inauthentic and almost embarrassed to call on customers, many of whom were my peers. This job lasted less than two years. I bounced between different sales positions with small companies afterwards and did equally poorly at each. After a few years I was ready to go back to treating clients.

Then I found a position with a mid-sized company that sold products to orthopedic surgeons using a soft-sell approach. This job utilized my knowledge of a product – an orthopedic knee brace - which I'd used in my athletic therapy work. Instead of selling in a direct way, the focus was on educating the doctors.

My big turning point was the moment I decided to change what selling meant to me. I became very successful in the orthopedic knee brace sales position. My success came from **redefining myself as an educator** to meet my clients' needs.

From that success, I developed the courage and qualifications to move to the big league - corporate sales - and found more obstacles to overcome there. My first corporate position was distribution sales. The focus was on managing a territory as a business – understanding gross profit margins, forecasting, price and cost analysis, negotiation skills, contract management etc. It utilized only a fraction of my healthcare expertise, which is where my strength lay, and being an educator was not a primary skill required for this role. Yikes! I was in over my head again.

I wanted so badly to be successful with this company and prove to myself that I could thrive in a sales career. Yet I struggled because I didn't like business, and that's what this job was all about! I wondered what I was missing. Why was I struggling so hard to do what others seemed to do effortlessly? Each time I moved to a new job, it got easier and I gained more skills, but it was as if I were constantly swimming upstream. I had my successes in this job, but I wasn't meeting my targets regularly. I was let go after four years, during a restructuring.

Once again, I considered leaving sales and business to find a new career. I took a step back and seriously considered if sales were the career for me. After some time off, I remembered how much I enjoyed my work with the knee brace company and wondered if there was a way to merge my healthcare background with a corporate sales position. At this point in my career, I had healthcare and hospital sales experience plus business experience. I started thinking about the large manufacturing companies I had competed against when selling knee braces, one of which was 3M. I applied to 3M and was hired in 1998 to their healthcare division. It was a perfect fit for me.

I was hired by Harvey Lockhart, one of the best managers I have ever worked for. He had confidence in me, my skills and abilities. He supported me, encouraged me, and challenged me to meet my full potential in my work. This position for me, under Harvey's tutelage, was the perfect condition for me to find success in sales. I developed a way of selling that made me a top-selling sales rep in my first year – and many successive years at 3M.

How did I do it? I found a way to sell that included my first revelation, seeing myself as an educator, combined with my strengths (healthcare knowledge, relationship-building skills, energy, professionalism and business acumen), and my interest and natural curiosity about my clients' work. With this approach I better understood their needs and how our products could help them meet *their* goals. Things finally started to click. I hit and surpassed my forecasts and found my success. **I had discovered a way to sell that didn't feel like selling** and that brought me success beyond what I believed possible. What made this so satisfying was that it was a win/win/win/win for me, 3M, my clients, and *their* clients. Woo Hoo!

With my new approach, I became one of the top-selling and award-winning sales reps in 3M's healthcare division. I had such great success I was eventually promoted to National Sales Manager.

I was an allied healthcare provider who had never imagined that one day I would have a successful business career in sales. I struggled for years with the concept of selling and finally found a way to overcome my negative perceptions and beliefs about it to create a selling process that worked for me and brought me success beyond anything I could have imagined.

It was time for me to integrate all that I learned to date and to give back in a way that resonated very strongly with me. For me it was getting back into the service industry, this time as a coach. I ended my career with 3M, completed a graduate program at Royal Roads University in Victoria, BC, and became certified as an executive coach. I started my own practice in 2006 doing business and corporate coaching.

It became a full circle moment for me as I was once again in the service industry, now equipped with the strongest sales expertise a person could have. One would think building my business and selling my services would be a snap. Not so. I have had to grow and learn even more about selling in this role.

To be honest, it took me, a seasoned sales veteran, awhile to become comfortable with selling *my* services. I was so distracted by all of the tasks involved with getting my business up and running I somehow lost myself and my confidence.

I realized that since it's *my* business, people who buy my services are truly buying a part of me. For me, that brought up the questions, "Am I worthy?" and "What is my value?" At the heart of being able to promote and sell what I have, I need to believe that I am good (at what I do), and that *I myself* have value; and by extension, my products and services do too. I was tackling so many new and first-time tasks involved in starting my own business, I found myself feeling less than competent. I was defining myself by what I was not strong at: accounting, book-keeping, IT, and social media marketing; rather than what I have mastered and excel at: relationship-building, health and wellness knowledge, business promotion, coaching, facilitation, and selling. The result of putting the focus back on what I do well was that my confidence to initiate and engage in authentic, joyful selling interactions returned.

If you are "sales reluctant," here are three steps you can take today to increase your confidence in promoting your service or products:

- **Redefine selling in a way that works for you.** In what ways are you and your business different from the sales image you dislike?

- **Know your strengths.** List five things you do well and that come easily to you. Next, what have others told you that you do well?

- **Put the focus on who you're serving.** Write, in two to three sentences, a statement that summarizes why a consumer should buy your product or use your service. Describe how you will add value or solve their specific problem.

Along the way I've learned that EVERY experience is valuable and important to getting to the next phase in life. They are not all easy or perfect, but I've found that my experiences are perfect for me *and* for what's coming for me! I once heard someone say, "The thing we struggle with most in our life is the thing we are meant to teach." I believe that to be true. And… Willy Loman, I am not!

Kimberly Martin *is a Certified Executive Coach and Principal of Martin Business Leadership, which creates custom business relationship strategies for health and wellness providers running small to medium-sized businesses. They'll help you grow your business, bring in new clients, solidify existing relationships, and have enjoyable, authentic, effortless selling interactions! To get their Free Special Report,* Top 10 Selling Mistakes Service Providers Make and How to Avoid Them! *visit www.MartinBusinessLeadership.com.*

The Dance of the Sacred Sensual Me

Leela Francis

I believe that life crafts a quilt of circumstances mapping out our destinies. Looking back, we see threads of the past stitching it all together. Discovering my calling, to re-unite women globally to our *sacred sensuality*, was this way for me. What I discovered through my own journey is that women's struggles in the developed world are different, yet related, to the struggles of women in developing countries. I also discovered that the obstacles we overcome in our own lives can be of tremendous value to our sisters worldwide.

My life quilt looked something like this. By age sixteen I had lost the fertility lottery, learning then that I would never be able to conceive. As for body image, I hated my body, dabbled in bulimia, and would have become anorexic if I could have resisted my love of food. And while I did confront my fears of the corporate world, I never felt good there. Instead I pursued work as a healer, leaving many material needs unfulfilled. So it seemed I was a washout financially too.

No motherhood, terrible body, and woeful finances. I didn't measure up in any of these departments, so my self-worth as a woman suffered miserably. I knew, however, in theory, that true success is determined by what's on the inside, not by how we look or by what we accomplish. My challenge was to turn theory into reality, despite all my apparent shortcomings weighing so heavily against me.

Further personal inquiry led me to ask: what is it that truly determines the success of a woman anyway? What fulfills her, resulting in a self-realized radiant glow, allowing her to look back one day on a life well lived? What is the essence of a woman, and how can we train ourselves and our culture to support that, rather than conform to a superficial, ill-fitting rendition of womanhood? And finally, how can I even stand to look at myself in the mirror and be at peace with my chronic self-criticism and questioning, when so many women in the world struggle to feed themselves and their families, to have their opinions matter, to have a choice to decide when to have sex, how to spend money, and whether they have a right to education?

My longing to make sense of these two radically different experiences of womanhood, the luxury of self-doubt, and the lack of essential rights and freedoms, pestered me. Little did I know this would become a creative force in my life.

My search for peace and self-acceptance led me, through my twenties, to study healing, yoga, and dance. I spent a lot of time in shamanic communities praying and learning. Not surprisingly, when I began teaching and practicing, I encouraged my students and clients to reconnect body, self, and soul to reach states of radiant self-worth - work I was intimately engaged in myself.

As my career and my aspirations grew, my life journey moved me from a spiritually nurturing, nature-vibrant environment on the Sunshine Coast of British Columbia, Canada, to the city of Vancouver, BC, where I believed I could grow and expand my following. Within six years of that move, despite fulfilling work, a family of stepsons to replace the lack of my own, a beautiful home, and a loving relationship, in my thirties I went through a major depression that changed my life. I didn't feel like dancing, being creative, or relating to the world. I was all dried up. Even teaching became a chore.

I tried many things including psychotherapy, dance therapy, inner child work, and homeopathy, but still I was depressed. After about a half year, my beloved and I traveled to Central America on vacation. While hiking by a river in a lush tropical jungle, I discovered a sense of home, peace, and belonging inhabiting me that I hadn't felt before, or not for a very long time. I felt embraced and cradled there. I wore little clothes and slept in a house with no walls. The contact of my skin with the elements and the immersion of all my senses within the natural world even as I slept, kindled a sensual aliveness and a self-love that were very unfamiliar.

This experience inspired my deeper inquiry into my feminine sensibilities and my connection to nature, affirming how desperately I longed to be lovingly reflected and fed by my environment. *This* quality of connection was clearly a non-negotiable requirement for my survival. Being surrounded by concrete, plastic, TV, and young male angst was leaving some important parts of me, what I now call my sacred sensuality, literally dying of starvation. I made the decision, then and there in the jungle, that I would gladly trade in forty more years of a less than fulfilling life for five years of *living fully now*, where the marriage of sensuality, spirituality, and creativity are prioritized. This decision ended up costing me my life as I knew it at the time. Though a necessary step for my survival, the loss of my relationship, my step-kids and my home were still excruciating.

Inspired and supported by the truth of my Sacred Sensual calling, to live and work in what was for me a lush and sensually abundant environment, I took steps to create that life for myself, based on a system of embodiment called The 5 Stages of VividExistence™, which are blessedly to thank for my success. My journey looked something like this:

I deeply **sensed** my craving to surround myself with a sensually nourishing environment.

I **grounded** that craving by working on a plan. I researched and applied to work in places where I could live, teach dance and yoga, and practice my healing work in a tropical setting.

Once offered a position, I **mobilized** into action by moving there. Let me tell you, this was not without extreme fears. Leaving the comforts of my life behind was terrifying, but knowing that my sensual essence would not be satisfied with anything less, I jumped into the unknown.

As wonderfully fulfilling as it was, I couldn't create a self-sustaining income in paradise. So I **harnessed** my resources by implementing business strategies that would help me to have a passive income and continue with my student following in the US and Canada while living in the tropics four-six months/year, i.e. designing and producing dance and meditation DVD's and CD's, contracting a virtual assistant and a marketer.

The previous four steps supported me to enjoy and **express** the truest essence of my sacred sensuality.

Once I awoke to the truth of my own sensual calling, I also became acutely aware of how disconnection from our sacred sensuality is epidemic in our world. Whether it's women who are being violated as a weapon of war in developing countries, or those of us in the developed world who have willingly sacrificed it in the interest of equality, success, and financial achievement, we are all at some level grieving a vital aspect of our aliveness, our sacred sensuality. And it is this very disconnection that is the crisis our planet now endures.

I learned that sacred sensuality, unique to each one of us, is independent of all the external trappings of career, children, physique, and culture. It is our intimate relationship to self and other as expressions of nature.

It seemed obvious to me that women coming together to support their sisters who have had their sacred sensuality horribly violated is a natural step towards rehabilitating our own and our sisters' sensual dignity. I founded *Vividly Woman*™, a global community of women leaders and women's circles devoted to the peace, prosperity, and freedom of all women, as a vehicle to marry our seemingly different, yet in truth, very similar issues. We gather in sacred circle to enjoy dance, nature re-connection, and creative ritual, and we've raised thousands of dollars for our sisters globally in the process.

My passion to support and nurture sacred sensuality for my sisters worldwide is an on-going reminder for me to nurture myself. I've learned that infusing my life daily with the sensual callings that nourish me is essential to nourish others. Having steps to identify, integrate, and embody these sensual callings is invaluable. The 5 Stages of VividExistence™: sense, ground, mobilize, harness, and express, are touchstones that keep me sensually on track.

Notice how these stages dance themselves in your life. Sense/savor what you long for. How can you ground/plan to actualize this sensual calling? Imagine yourself mobilizing into action. Now how are you going to harness/sustain this abundance, and finally, enjoy yourself expressing the fullest radiance of this sensual calling?

My sensual calling is a passionate expression of my life journey thus far to live in radiant sensual abundance. The circling community of *Vividly Woman*™ is a testament to that journey. Dancing onward, we tend the flames of a global paradigm, embracing women's *sacred sensuality*, essential to wholeness, peace, and prosperity for all.

Leela Francis is the founder of VividExistence™ *and* Vividly Woman™. *She facilitates events internationally, inspiring groups and individuals to turn up the volume on their radiance in service of all beings and the planet. Her retreats, workshops, and audiovisual products are enjoyed by thousands across North America, and she has raised thousands of dollars for women survivors of war. Visit www.VividlyWoman.com and receive your Free recording,* Sacred Sensuality and the 5 Stages of VividExistence.

140 Boxes...
More Than a Ton of
Ancient History

Virginia Fischer

In January of 2003, one and a half years after moving into my town home in Phoenix, Arizona, I decided to locate all my yet-unpacked boxes in my new home. Even after having help unpacking right after my move, a count revealed a mind boggling fact: I still had 140 boxes yet to be unpacked. When I first moved into my 1300-square-foot home, the entire space felt and looked like one solid box, minus space for living and dining room furniture, and my brother Mike's and my beds.

My mother's and my furniture, clothes, pictures, and favorite kitchen gadgets were all brought to my town home in a very large moving van. Thanks go to my eldest brother, Bob, who directed the movers, while I attempted to keep boxes going into the correct rooms. I had taken care of my mother until she needed twenty-four hour nursing care, so my home became the repository of her life history and furniture, as her room at the nursing home was too small.

In January 2003, Mike moved out, so I decided to confine the just-moved-in look to one bedroom, whose door could be closed should company come calling. However, I soon discovered that ALL 140 remaining boxes were filled with paper!

Letting Go Was All It Took ... or So I Thought

My sister Linda coached me from her home on the East Coast: just decide on five or six major topics and sort the paper into the chosen categories. Easy to say, but not at all easy to do. There was little organization to what was in those 140 boxes. Yes, I had designed and created workshop materials which fit neatly into one box, and another five boxes contained article clippings, newspapers, and magazines. However, that left 134 boxes yet to be sorted.

2003 Major Life Changes Afoot

In May 2003, I was fired from one of the worst jobs I'd ever had. However, my mother was on hospice and I had intended to tough out that job until later in the year. Now I decided to devote full time to the coach training courses at CoachU. Happily for my mother, she made her transition in August, three months after I lost my job.

This is Doable

After my mother's Memorial Service in late September, my niece, Ann, came to my home to view the sorting room. She looked at the boxes piled four or five high in multiple rows, the nine foot long table covered with boxes, stacks of paper, and with an encouraging voice said, "Aunt Virginia, this is doable, this can be done." Her well-chosen words ignited hope in my heart. I needed encouragement to keep going, as it was tough dealing with all that disorganized paper.

While Bob took some time before returning East to go through some of the boxes of Mother's papers, Linda helped me work on some of my boxes. What a huge blessing! It really made a difference to get help clearing out some more old memories.

After Mother's passing, I had no drive or energy to deal with any of the boxes. There were months at a time when walking into the "sorting room" was next to impossible. It was a very dense atmosphere, as I didn't know when I would open a box with memories I hadn't yet resolved. Progress seemed very, very slow.

January 2005 Rolls In and The Sorting Room Morphs

In December 2004, I completed my CoachU life coach training and decided to again focus on my boxes and decluttering. I moved as many of the remaining boxes as I possibly could into the bedroom closet. This way it wasn't such an assault on my senses to look at or walk into the room.

Linda Comes West to Help Sort

In May 2005, Linda came to help sort and to visit Sedona's beauty and ambience. She helped me set up my work by going through fifty-sixty boxes and sorting their contents into six major categories.

Clutter Free Class to the Rescue!

In June 2005, one of my CoachU instructors started a teleclass called, "Learn To Be Clutter Free." I signed up for an eight-week class and then repeated it again. It was really powerful to meet other people who were working on letting go of their "stuff," i.e. clutter. Taking a questionnaire before the class began, I realized that the clutter in the "sorting room" kept spilling out into the rest of the house each time I took something out of the room into another part of the house. The files or boxes would sit on top of a table until I became motivated again to continue that project or box. What a de-motivator!

My niece, Ann, was working on her own decluttering in her home and periodically would email me an article she had received from Fly Lady, an online decluttering service. She knew what I was experiencing at my end, since she had seen my huge task.

Humor Helps Heal the Heart

During the Clutter Free class, I made some interesting comments on clutter:

"Being on the planet for untold eons, I now have the perfect vantage point to view the clutter in my life. The 'perfect' vantage point is that age carries both seniority and height. I am both older and higher than the clutter, so no matter how great the pile, I am always at a distinct advantage. And I can walk, talk, and make decisions. Clutter usually grows roots and stays totally put. It obediently moves to wherever I place it next.

Clutter very skillfully decreases my energy level every time I look at it. It even taunts me if I try to avoid seeing its unmistakable presence."

Periodic Victories

As things progressed, I became able to keep the kitchen and dining room clutter-free. The biggest payoff for me was to feel the difference energetically. The clutter-free space was peaceful, inviting, even nurturing. I loved seeing the counter tops free of piles of magazines, newspapers, or books. It felt great. Noticing the energy shift that occurred when these areas became clutter-free was what kept me going. I was able to anchor these feelings and translate it into the sorting room. I was able to visualize the room without the boxes or the clutter.

The Sorting Room Renamed

It became obvious to me that the words "sorting room" had a negative energy, so I decided to call it my "Creativity Room." The new name felt lots better. However, there were still quite a few boxes remaining in my Creativity Room.

In September 2008, a student from a class I'd taught volunteered to help me work on this never-ending project. I welcomed her with both gratitude and awe. What she was stepping into was not a simple project to be finished in forty-five days or less.

After she had helped me for about a month, I offered to give her spiritual counseling and affirmative prayer in exchange for her time. She liked this exchange, and together we made regular progress on decreasing the contents of the Creativity Room.

At the end of January 2009, I was able to move my bedroom into the Creativity Room. There still remain some boxes to be pared down, but only three or four boxes need to be sorted into the six major categories. Several additional boxes already sorted or yet to be pared down reside in my outside storage.

Lessons Learned From 140 Boxes of Paper

Keeping information and unfinished projects for as long as I did left many unresolved strands of threads tugging at my energy. This depleted me and often caused me to get distracted from doing things that had more value to me.

I can only say that if I were starting this now, it would be done much differently and hopefully much more sanely and clearly.

Decluttering Words of Wisdom:

If you have piles and/or boxes of paper, here are 7 Vital Steps to Victorious Decluttering:

• Set up or develop a foolproof system to limit your inflow of paper, unsubscribe to junk mail, get off email lists, etc.

• Develop your sorting system, but keep it SIMPLE. The more complex it becomes, the more likely it is to break down. It must meet YOUR needs, not someone else's.

• Hire a willing helper… and the sooner the better.

- Really learn to let go of paper and "stuff." The Internet has all the answers you'll ever need.

- Learn to "bounce" back when "failure" appears to occur. Life happens, but you get to direct your life however you choose.

- Never, Never, Never, Never Give Up!

- Build your Faith, and Believe in yourself and the difference you do make in the world everyday. This is highly strategic and self-loving.

Don't wait until you have 140 boxes of "stuff" cluttering up your space and your life!

Virginia Fischer, CEO of Living Well Lifestyle, LLC, empowers her clients to create the lifestyle of their dreams. By clarifying their life passions through courageous living, clients take action to live the lifestyle of their dreams. Virginia's articles can be found at online article directories. For tips and tools to enjoy a healthy, prosperous life and gain greater wisdom visit www.LivingWellLifestyleLLC.com and download her Free article, 8 Essential Lifestyle Choices Impacting Your Life.

Are You Credit Worthy?

~⌒

Nancy Cotter

Not long ago my world came crashing down... financially, emotionally, and spiritually.

My husband was in a real funk after more than thirty years of owning a mushroom and produce business. A series of setbacks that began in the wake of 9/11 were taking a major toll on us. From customers going out of business, to food scares, out-of-control fuel prices, and an inability to raise market prices, we were struggling to keep our heads above water. I was no longer married to "Mr. Blue Skies and Sunshine." The smiling, optimistic sweetheart I had married so many years ago was now all doom and gloom.

As I did my best to cut expenses and help my husband search for solutions, the other shoe began to drop. One by one, tragedies seemed to come our way. By Thanksgiving I had attended too many funerals, broken two fingers, and was nursing my dog after a vicious attack by another dog.

Earlier that year, my sister was well on her way to building a successful credit restoration company in Kentucky. She knew we were seeking alternatives and approached us with a generous offer. She would train me and provide whatever help I needed to set up my own business as a satellite of hers.

It sounded interesting so I flew out that summer for a visit. We spent the week in training and reviewing her system. I was excited for her and pleased with the results she was getting for her clients. It was a great opportunity, but I was not ready to step up and take a risk. So, I flew home and returned to my corporate job. I held back.

Things got a bit better for my husband's company and we managed to keep going. His mood improved, though I could tell he was covering up his concerns. He's good at that.

By the fall it was pretty much business as usual until one night in late October. The phone rang as we were heading for bed – never a good omen. I could tell immediately by my husband's voice that something terrible had happened.

His sister was clinging to life in a hospital in North Carolina following a horrific accident. Her husband of forty years, our brother-in-law, was dead. He had been killed instantly along with their two dearest friends. Those friends were the parents of our nephew's wife and part of our family as well.

Reeling with shock and disbelief, I booked a flight from Philadelphia and was in North Carolina the next day. My husband's younger sister, my life-long friend, did the same. We joined our two nephews and their families, bonding in grief and despair.

For a week we kept a constant vigil, taking turns with our precious patient. We talked to doctors and made funeral arrangements for the three we had lost. We attended services and plotted the course for our sister's recovery. With plans decided, we flew home to put things in place. Our help would be needed at a later date. But the following week found us back in North Carolina with our nephews, making plans of a different sort. Their mother had passed. Our dear sister was gone. We were left to pick up the pieces.

The final services were over by Thanksgiving. It was a pitiful holiday season. I had plenty of time to reflect and grieve as my dog and I recuperated together – him from his surgery and me with my broken fingers and emotions. I felt hollow and depleted.

With all of my heart I now knew how fragile life is. Every moment is precious. It can end in an instant. I began questioning myself and my beliefs. I began opening to change.

I was thankful that my sister-in-law and brother-in-law had lived in their mountain paradise for almost three years before their untimely death. They knew the joy of living a life they loved. They had faced their fears and made a choice to follow their dreams.

They were approaching sixty when they made their decision. I was already fifty-three. My dreams had been nagging me my whole life. What was I waiting for? The clock was ticking and it was time to take action. I repressed my fear, called my sister in Kentucky, and accepted her offer. But little did I know, as I built my credit consulting business, that those fears would re-surface and keep me paralyzed until I finally faced them head on.

You see, my dreams aren't of riches and fame. What has tugged at me is finding a way to help others find peace and happiness. Yet my fear of failure, ridicule, and criticism made me feel extremely vulnerable. I was afraid to step out of my comfort zone. But I was determined. I had a burning desire to live up to my dream. I felt like this was my last chance to get it right. I knew there was a way to move beyond the fear – I just had to find it. So I became a voracious student, talked to coaches, attended seminars, found websites and resources. I consumed books, CDs and DVDs.

I pulled back from marketing my business to pursue my quest. When people I loved didn't understand and voiced their disapproval, I stood my ground and kept on. When I was criticized and accused of failure, I cried for days but continued on. When I came up against such powerful fear that I thought I was dying, somehow I found strength to carry on. After months of seeking and learning and trying, I was exhausted and gave up control. That's when the breakthrough came.

When I surrendered my own will I finally saw myself without illusions, and my fear began to dissolve. What was revealed seems so obvious now that I have to smile. I had read about similar experiences. I had studied science, psychology and spirituality, but never fully understood. I had to experience it for myself and reveal my true Self, before I could move on.

The irony is that my fear was created by my mind to protect me. Science has shown that our brains are programmed to hold onto negative input, no matter how trivial. This evolved as a way to warn us of potential danger. Unfortunately, positives are overshadowed and our perceptions become distorted. The negative accumulates and can easily convince us we are unworthy.

I found out that I was my own worst enemy because I craved the approval and acceptance of others. Instead of following my own heart and trusting myself, I allowed false negative perceptions to hold me back. In order to succeed I had to re-program my thoughts. This experience is not unique to me, but I share it with you because of what I learned as a result. It addresses the question I posed as the title of this chapter.

Our society is driven by the fear of "not enough." We have convinced ourselves there's not enough time, money, and resources. We are so caught up in this misperception that we judge ourselves and others by false measures and focus on financial identities. We simply don't know who we are anymore. That confusion causes a lot of unnecessary suffering. I found a way to alleviate some of this pain and confusion, and believe that's why I've been so compelled to experience what I have, to arrive here at this moment. The dream that nagged me my entire life is now pulling me along.

I believe finding peace of mind with your finances and yourself is connected to answering the title question, with no illusions about who you *think* you are. It requires a clear-eyed assessment of who you *really* are. This means removing blinders and excuses; it requires responsibility and action.

To ease your mind a bit, I will tell you right now that we are ALL credit worthy.

Improving your financial credit and sense of self-worth begins with knowing exactly where you stand and why. Unless you identify core problems and issues, you will never overcome them to reach your full potential. With a solid understanding, you can put a plan into action for life-changing results.

I know it may sound difficult, but it's really not so tough. My journey of trials and tribulations led me to discover some amazing tools and resources. I put them to good use and created a user-friendly way to help you get the peace of mind you need and deserve. If I overcame what held me back, I know you can too. It starts with being open to change.

So I pose the question to you: *Are you credit worthy?*

As I close, I want to thank two special spirits who inspired me to live my dream. Their decision to live theirs in the mountains of North Carolina gave our family many happy memories we would not have shared otherwise. I know they are smiling now at this new adventure.

Hugs and kisses to you, Cheri and Tom.

Nancy Cotter is a Personal Credit Coach who will empower you to take charge of your credit and sense of self-worth to get the peace of mind you need and deserve. Through education, inspiration, and motivation, Nancy provides the resources and tools for life-changing results. Get her Special Free Report, The Top 3 Things YOU MUST DO NOW to Avoid or Survive a Personal Credit Crisis, *at her website www.apluscreditcoach.com.*

INSPIRATION

The first great gift we can bestow on others is a good example.
~ Thomas Morell

When the Rain Falls

Paula Morand

When the rainy season comes to Liberia, the villagers say the gushing wall of water is actually God, who is spilling unending tears of sadness for His people.

These heavy rains pepper the ground like a hail of bullets, mirroring the bullet holes that are visible in every building.

Does God cry tears of sadness? If He does, He would certainly be justified in crying for Liberia. The West African country survived fifteen years of civil unrest with rebel factions and six long years at war under the cruel and corrupt regime of Charles Taylor (now in exile). Children were abandoned, orphaned, and often forced into soldiery or prostitution; the women were raped and villages destroyed.

However, in the past four years, having a relatively stable government, foreign involvement, and a strong UN presence, these resilient people are beginning to hope for peace. They have the will to rebuild, the heart to forgive, and the soul to survive. Despite everything that has been stripped away, these communities are ready to put their experiences of past abuse, exploitation and starvation behind them. They don't just want to survive, they wanted to *flourish*. But how does one thrive in the face of such extreme trauma?

As I stood in that African jungle under a rough thatched porch and watched the fierce rain, I remembered a rainy season in my own life, a time when I also felt unending tears of sadness. Back then my survival also depended on my own determination and resilience, not only to cope, but also to nurture the hope that I, just like these villagers, would flourish someday.

I was twenty-three when I married a man nine years my senior. He had an exciting career in the hospitality industry and we were fortunate to travel and live in some exciting places. Thoughtful and sensitive, experienced and mature, he seemed prepared to take care of my every need. We built the home of our dreams in the country and when I became pregnant with our son, my joy was truly complete. I was going to be the best wife, the best mother, and we were going to have the best life ever. That is, until a series of events crashed through my picket fence and destroyed all my dreams.

During my pregnancy, my husband was threatened at knifepoint while managing a hotel on New Year's Eve. I was blithely unaware of my husband's underlying struggle with depression and other mental issues, but the assault was the first crack in the dam. This traumatic event, along with the strong medication he was prescribed to cope with it, pushed his paranoia into full blown psychosis.

He was unable to return to the hotel and his position, thus forcing him to take another job with a different hotel in the city where I was raised. We were moving once again, and as quickly as we had moved into our dream home, we were trading it in and seemingly taking a huge step backward.

I was home alone one day, playing with my ten month old son when the phone rang.

"Is your husband going to kill me?" a woman's voice cried, after I said hello. I recognized her voice even though she was screaming hysterically, as she was an employee of my husband.

"What is she talking about?" I thought. Stunned, I answered, "What?" "You heard me," she continued. "Is your husband going to kill me?"

I convinced myself the bewildering conversation had been a prank until a short time later when a policeman arrived at the door. He said that my husband, the man I trusted, loved and admired so much, had threatened to kill not one, but three female co-workers and was now locked in a psychiatric ward.

I never knew the face of mental illness until I saw my husband at the hospital that day. I was twenty-six years old when the man I'd known as a kind, loving husband, my best friend, and my inspiration, evaporated into thin air. He never returned. I looked in his eyes, blank and unresponsive, and felt as though the last four years of my life were wiped out in an instant as a stranger now inhabited his body.

I quickly realized that I would have to assume full responsibility for what was happening in my home and with my beautiful baby boy. My fears about being able to rebuild my life increased. Six months later I sustained severe whiplash in a car accident that occurred just after dropping off my son at daycare. I had recently lost my job and decided to start my own business, so now I had no employee benefits to assist me in my recovery. With little assistance from anyone in my life at the time, I felt abandoned and alone, with the threat of becoming homeless with my young child looming over my head.

Heavily medicated, my husband spent the next five years in and out of psychiatric wards. Diagnosed with bi-polar depression with schizophrenic tendencies, he told me he couldn't love me, and that he wasn't able to be the father that he wanted to be. At that point we both knew that the relationship that once was so exciting had now become frightening. Afraid for my life and that of our son's, I had no choice but to move on. My husband and I managed to struggle with this new reality for the sake of our son. No matter how angry I was about the situation, I came to the realization that it was so much worse for him. Mental illness, you see, is a cruel affliction that not only attacks and destroys the person, but fragments the whole family and knows no boundaries.

During this difficult transition period I felt that I had to put on a brave face when visiting my parents, who expected me to be strong. While they cared for my young son inside the house, I would head for their backyard pool and dive deep down into the water and scream. I would come up gasping for air, and dive down over and over, screaming under the water where they couldn't hear me. *"Why, God? Why have you let life suffocate me like this? Turn back the clock. Please fix this. Can You hear my cries? Are You crying too, or do You even care?"* When I had fully screamed out my frustrations in the pool, I told them my eyes were red from the chlorine.

It turns out that God did hear me, and He did care about my situation, although it took one step at a time to see it. I found success and confidence in my role as an entrepreneur and with hard work my company grew and flourished. My beautiful boy kept me sane and he was my inspiration to keep going.

I once asked my husband how he had reached that deep place of hopelessness, that place where one sees not even a sliver of light. He told me, "It's like being thrown in a torrential thunderstorm. Darkness completely envelops you in an instant, without a moment's notice, and drowns out any other sound or light from getting in." Much like the torrential rains I experienced in Liberia.

I asked him, "But you believe in God, don't you? Can't you ask Jesus to heal you?"

He would only turn away from me and say, "I don't think He wants to heal me."

After many attempts, he finally succeeded in ending his struggle with mental illness and overdosed a few years ago in his parents' home. I was broken-hearted that, unlike the hopeful Liberian people I met recently, he was never able to believe that better days were possible.

Does God shed unending tears of sadness for His people? I believe He does, not just for the tragic experiences we endure, but also when we fail to look up and see that sunshine and new life will surely follow the rain if we choose not to give up. Through forgiveness and reconciliation, we can let our sadness and suffering go and see that life is really good.

Ten years ago I met a wonderful man with similar life experiences, who not only adopted my son as his own, but has since blessed me with another child. On the foundations of a life razed by the pelting rain, we continue to build our new family. Over the years the process of healing has taught me integral life lessons that have helped me live a life of joy, and control the story which was once in control of me. I have learned to embrace the rain. Let it come so that it may nourish and bring new life, new hope and allow me to appreciate the sunshine that follows.

Paula Morand is passionate about championing the needs of others. From her Canadian roots, to the mountains of Central Asia, the street vendors of Cuba, and the jungles of Africa, Paula lives an enthusiastic adventure that sees lives changed. Founder/CEO of JumpStart 720 International Inc., Paula is an enthusiastic Professional Speaker, Business Consultant and Leadership Coach who inspires individuals, businesses and communities to make positive change. For your Free Life Changer Checklist, visit www.Jumpstart720.com or www.PaulaMorand.com.*

Growing Up After Fifty: It's Never Too Late to Bloom

Tomar Levine

"There is nothing sadder than an individual who has reached the age of fifty and still has not engaged life, for then he or she must face [two] dilemmas at once. Such a person must prepare for the second stage of life without ever having completed the first ... The only way to deal with this is through an accelerated growing-up process."

> - *BALANCING HEAVEN AND EARTH: A MEMOIR*
> ROBERT A. JOHNSON AND JERRY M. RUHL

I was already past fifty when I read, with a jolt, these words of the Jungian analyst Robert Johnson. In a way it was a relief to have my condition acknowledged so poignantly – this condition that I had rarely, if ever, seen described. Nonetheless, his words saddened, even shamed me, until I reached the last sentence. Then I felt hope and joy, and again the odd sensation of being recognized and described by an unknown stranger. For I knew that I had, in fact, embarked on the very process he named as the only solution to my dilemma: I was in the process of growing up.

As a child I was precocious and gifted, won prizes for drawing and writing in my teens, but exasperated my family by being thin-skinned and "too sensitive." I was introverted, lacked robustness and had trouble coping. My parents handled me with proverbial kid gloves and allowed me to shy away from challenges because of the fuss I made. As a result, I never built the confidence that only comes from meeting challenges and overcoming obstacles. In my twenties, for my first apartment, my brother gave me a sign that read, "Girl Genius." And into my thirties and forties I continued to play that role, forgetting to grow up – or at least putting it off – and off.

Delayed Adulthood

Several factors contributed to my delayed adulthood. Being an artist, single and childless, I bypassed the rites of passage and responsibilities of most adults. My Depression-era parents' version of responsibility made adulthood look unappealing anyway. Looking young, acting young, thinking and feeling young helped create the illusion that time was barely passing, and aging did not apply to me. Finally, having a small amount of family money – enough to barely get by on – was a double-edged sword. On the one hand it allowed me to paint, write, read, and pursue the spiritual studies I was drawn to. On the other, not having to earn much income allowed me to act out my insecurities by rejecting ambition, not taking risks, and living a far smaller, more protected life than another part of me longed for.

Hiding my light under a bushel was never my plan. I wanted to be a recognized artist. Hiding one's light is simply what happens when fear is stronger than the desire to have one's light seen and to add value to the world. I exhibited my art for years, maintaining a miniscule career that reflected my comfort zone. But when I discovered a spiritual calling, the heat was turned up on my inner conflict and my suffering intensified!

Now it was not just for my own glory, but for something greater that I wanted my light to shine. I knew I had something to share that filled me and could inspire others – if only I could find the form. I searched for my true work the way others seek true love. Many times I thought I'd found it, yet I continued to fear risk and rejection even more than I yearned to be of service. I remained a perpetual student long after I should have been teaching, as I waited to be invited to take my place onstage. Like a corked volcano, I was full of blocked energy. I tried to convince myself that being invisible was more spiritual than releasing my life force, but secretly I felt shame. I feared I would waste my life and the gifts I had been given.

Turning Point

My life is different now. I've finally found the work I was searching for. Coaching combines what I love most – writing, teaching, art, as well as helping people, individually and in groups, find what *their* soul is looking for.

I discovered that, far from being an "over-gifted underachiever," I'm a late bloomer – and that part of my path and purpose is to bloom late. What excites me now is helping others bloom in any season, for I know firsthand that it's never too late to bloom!

What changed for me?

- Ordinary life provided challenges: "parenting" my aging parents, dealing with their deaths, returning to graduate school after fifty, and more.

- I worked on myself for years and healed, matured, developed. And I consciously dissolved many fear-based, self-rejecting beliefs (*very* important!).

- I came to a turning point, followed my guidance, and made a commitment to myself.

Confronting Fear

A time came when I realized I was running out of tomorrows. Money was becoming finite too. I had a "lightbulb" moment and felt guided to become a coach. And I promised myself: *"This time, no matter what, no matter how scared I feel, I'm not going to give up!"*

Taking that oath was probably the single most important turn in my road. As I ventured into new territory, further from what felt safe, there were many times when I had to remind myself of it. Many times my friends had to remind me that I was more than my fear, and that I could soothe my frightened inner child. I didn't stop having fear, but I gradually learned not to let my fear stop me.

Notice that "scared" becomes "sacred" by just shifting one letter – the "c." By shifting how I *see* my life, I change my whole reality.

When I'm scared my attention is narrow and fear fills my screen. When I focus on what I experience as sacred, my vision widens. The fear grows smaller, and finally disappears.

Where I place my attention makes all the difference, especially when I remember to return, again and again, to my inspiration, to what lights up my soul. That light has been waiting a long time for me to put it first. It has been waiting for me to grow up.

It is this connection to my inner light that helps me take my next steps. The steps in themselves are sometimes daunting, but the inner alignment lifts my energy, and that's where the magic happens. Synchronicities abound and I am invariably drawn to just what I need: the information, the helper, the next wonderful kindred spirit to co-create with.

Start with Inspiration

If you want one place to start, tune into your source of guidance and find what lights up your soul. This will give you the direction forward and the power to persevere. You have that source of guidance within you, even if you think you don't.

How do you find the passion that lights you up? First – and this is crucial – *lock your inner critic in the closet!* He's the one whose job it is to tell you what's wrong with you and with what you love, and his input will snuff out possibilities. (You'll have to do this more than once!)

Then, in this peaceful, critic-free zone, let yourself remember what has ever brought you joy, excitement, or fulfillment – any pursuit, talent, or activity in which you have used your gifts, made a contribution, felt an inner "yes!" – or any fantasy that has beckoned, or any way that your soul has ever felt called. When one of these asks for more attention, turn to it and give your imagination freedom to play, for imagination and inspiration are linked.

Here are some ways to create that peaceful space that invites inspiration:

1. **Take steps**, literally. I find walking in nature – and for me that means a city park – opens my creative flow. The regular rhythmic movement with its left-right balance is conducive to insight and intuition. Being in nature also opens our energy field and nourishes us energetically. Start with an intention, a question, or a focus and just walk and let your thoughts flow. (And bring a way to capture them.)

2. **Cultivate stillness.** Quiet time, sitting alone – for me at night by lamp light, with a journal nearby – is a time of enormous productivity, in which ideas and answers are free to arise. Ask yourself a

question and wait, listen, be receptive. Then write down whatever comes. It may be words, images, impressions, or memories – don't judge it. Just stay with the thread and it will lead you somewhere fruitful.

2. **Cultivate, in and around yourself, an environment that is inspiration-friendly.** If you don't live alone, carve out some time and place just for you, and cherish it. Beautiful, meaningful objects help create sacred space.

Your inner self can become your greatest source of nourishment. Honor it, especially if you are looking for your soul's expression and are longing to bloom. For it is there that you will find the seeds of your blooming.

And above all, remember: it's *NEVER too late to bloom!*

Tomar Levine is a Life Purpose, Career, and Creativity Coach, speaker, writer, and artist. She inspires and empowers people to listen to their inner self, reclaim their dreams, and flower in any season. She knows it's never too late for you to discover your purpose, your true path and true work, and to fulfill your creative potential. To claim your Free Report on Why This May Be Your Best Time to Bloom, *visit www.YourTimeToBloom.com.*

How Do I Get Out of Here?

Scott G. Cunningham

Looking back nearly fifty or so years, I recognize that without the mercy of God so many things could have happened differently. I'm wondering how I can compress a lifetime of pain, turmoil, and dysfunction into just one chapter. After sharing my experience, you might wonder where God's mercy was. Did God allow these life-altering events, or were they for my destruction by an unseen enemy? It matters not now, for this once long-time captor, through the gift of time, has become an experience and expression of power, mercy, and grace.

Our words and actions can have such profound, immediate, and long lasting effects on others. All too often we hear accounts of people who were so traumatized or bullied by someone that they became a desperate soul, unequipped to properly resolve or heal their pain. Sometimes they harm themselves and at different times others may fall victim. I have walked this precipice on numerous occasions and rather than inflicting pain or retribution on others, I looked inwardly, assuming the problem was with me. I must admit that I did hurt and cause pain to my parents as well as those closest to me along this journey called life. Even though I know now they did nothing wrong, subconsciously I blamed my parents for not protecting me better. As for those I called friends, in my mind I figured there must be something wrong with them if they liked me.

Have you ever been in a near death situation? Numerous times I have encountered people and experienced events where a split second decision and the mercy of God determined life rather than death. As a struggling teenager I made several legitimate attempts to commit suicide. This is usually such a personal and private matter, you may wonder why I'm addressing these attempts to end my own life, but bear with me. As a teenager, I suffered with constant depression, a terrible sleeping disorder, and a horrible rollercoaster of emotions in my mind. Like many teenagers, I tried numerous sports, music, many social and school activities, drugs, and even church to counterbalance my feelings, yet still there was no internal resolution. Because of these continuous challenges, I was convinced that I was a misfit, defective, and that something was wrong with me. During those early years and at times later in life, I pushed the envelope way past logic or common sense, all the while carefully calculating the limits and boundaries wherein I thought I was safe.

In 1973, I recognized a great void in my soul and asked Jesus to be my Lord. In spite of the events of my early childhood, I accepted that God really did love me. I soon recognized the mercy of God that had kept me alive through those tumultuous years. For example, I remember being thirteen and putting a rope around my neck and kicking the chair out from under my feet. I guess the rope breaking was not a fluke. In my thirties, my mother informed me that while pregnant, the Army doctors told her I was stillborn and recommended an abortion.

In the Bible, Hosea 4:6 states, "My people are destroyed for lack of knowledge," or vision. Finally, I was gaining direction and hope. I wish I could say that all my problems were resolved, but that was not the case. Though I found inner peace, I still needed inner healing. Overcomers are not always greeted by a prize. Sometimes we simply arrive at a point where we can see clearly enough to find new vision, direction, purpose, or the ability to move on to the next path or obstacle.

I cannot adequately address the numerous, serious and life- altering betrayals I experienced. The accumulation of events in my life reached critical mass and in the 80's I began a thirteen-year downward spiral. Often I thought about Job's difficult trials. Everywhere I turned and every path I walked was dark and dangerous. In 1993, I found myself on a creek bank with a loaded, cocked Ruger, safety off, in my mouth, with my finger on the trigger, wondering how I had arrived there. At times, all my calls to the Lord seemed unanswered until that day on the bank when I cried out asking why He had previously revealed Himself to me, only then to seemingly abandon me. Then I heard the Lord say it was so I would have an anchor to hold onto during the storms He knew I would encounter.

For years, doctors and therapists told me that I was manic-depressive and that drugs would fix the problem, yet I would not accept this. Some might ask, "Why did God not just heal you?" He certainly could have, but sometimes we have to walk through the storm to reach the calm. Therefore, I continued to dig and search for answers. I finally found a doctor who took a sincere interest in my mess of a life and helped me to address the root problem. He helped me understand that being raped repeatedly between the ages of five to six was not my fault and that at the age of thirty- something I was still suffering from Post Traumatic Stress Disorder (PTSD). Finally, it all made sense.

It is most difficult to comprehensively explain the real, ugly, and lingering effects of rape to someone who has not experienced this. For example, I have witnessed firsthand wounded soldiers choppered in from Vietnam, and though I have talked at length with many veterans who survived combat, there is no way I can see it through their eyes. I cannot possibly comprehend their trauma of war. Though our experiences are quite different, the effects are quite similar. You can cover it up, block, or even ignore the psychological injury for many years, but it is in you and eventually requires careful attention. The truth of the matter is we can try to convince ourselves that we are okay, but we know that we need healing and help to overcome the effects of the injury to our soul and spirit.

I believe that low self-esteem and the debilitating, life-altering effects of PTSD led to most of the situations in which I found myself. Oftentimes I could hear my father saying, "If you are not in a pool hall at two in the morning, then you can't get hit over the head with a pool cue at two in the morning." Our choices will reap fruit, either good or bad.

For years I pondered what my life could or would have been like had it not been altered in such a manner. Would I have been as rebellious or troubled? Would I have done so many abnormal things? In reality, these were just vain thoughts. I could not alter the past, only the future. My choices really were quite simple. I could remain a victim, as is often the case with many survivors of traumatic events, I could stay bound in mind and spirit, unable to escape the shadows of guilt, shame and trauma, or I could begin the journey of healing. Many years ago in an effort to obtain some resolution about my childhood trauma and thinking it would be cathartic, I wrote a letter to the perpetrator. This was so difficult. I was not seeking retribution, nor was I looking to cause grief or even pain. I only longed to hear the words, "I am sorry." They never came.

In all honesty, I believe the restoration I continue to experience is a result of mercy, desire, determination, and others' love. I have so longed to be whole inside. My relationship with Jesus Christ is dynamic, growing, legitimate, powerful, and healing. At the same time, for almost forty years I was the victim of PTSD. In order to not be marginalized, I had to overcome this merciless crippler of the spirit, soul, and body. I have known for years that God had a higher calling for me than to be "road kill." I found the necessary help I required through many sources, including a doctor who compassionately provided sound guidance, and by accepting the value and importance of friendships. I am learning to accept that I do not have to be perfect. My greatest strength is my knowledge of the love, care, peace, and presence of the Holy Spirit in my life. By Jesus' description, He is the Comforter and the one who accompanies us on our journey. Thankfully, He continues to lead, comfort, and guide me. Last, but most certainly not least, is the unconditional love of my precious soul mate and wife, Denise. Her attention, love, and care draw out the very best of my heart and help me to stay whole. All combined, these elements continue to heal, strengthen and guide my soul, enabling me to keep rising above those indelible pains and truly walk the life of an Overcomer.

Scott G. Cunningham is a minister, missionary, and author of One Christ One Body, *which focuses on Christians' obligations as Christ's body. He founded Integrity Mission Ministry to promote and generate support for effective ministries. This book allows a view into a most personal life- altering event and his quest and journey for healing. To receive Scott's Free Report,* The Rest of the Story, *please visit Scott's website www.OvercomerAnthology.com.*

A Time of Grief ~
A Time of Peace

Catherine VanWetter, MSW

I remember so vividly hearing those dreadful, life-changing words on the snowy drive back home. As if in a dream state, those haunting words would echo in my ears for years to come, as my mother calmly said, breaking the heavy silence, "See that bright star in the sky? That's your sister." I didn't comprehend the words that were coming out of her mouth. There was so much that I didn't understand about those last six months when my sister started to get sick, since I was only a child of seven.

At times this memory has been so vivid that I can clearly hear my mother's voice and relive the exact location where she told me that my beloved sister Connie had, at the tender age of four, died of leukemia. Trauma does that. It leaves a visceral memory in every cell of your body. The sights, sounds, smells, and physical surroundings become acutely highlighted. Years can pass and unless resolved and released from the body, the traumatic incident will continue to catapult one back into the moment it originally occurred.

Before Connie died, our home was solemn and tense. Dad didn't talk much and Mom was either depressed or angry. Having no one to talk to, I lost myself in the mountains, retreating deep into the beautiful ponderosa, seeking solace and peace. The mountains entertained me for hours as I hiked with my dear dog companion, Pierre, passing waterfalls and making forts out of fallen trees. I was a loner and didn't have many friends. It felt as though no one understood what I was experiencing. I cried a lot and was made fun of at school by my so-called friends. I almost flunked first and second grade because I couldn't read or write. I felt like an empty shell full of grief and sadness. I used to listen to the coyotes howl at night, and in some strange way I felt such a resonance with them. Their howls mirrored the grief and sadness that I kept deep inside me. They gave it a voice. Though their cries scared me, I also felt a sense of relief when I heard them.

My sister died Dec. 23, 1961. Mom and Dad were with her at the hospital when she turned her head away from them and took her last breath. I didn't get to say goodbye to her, nor did I go to her funeral. I suppose my parents felt that it was best for me not to go. Yet I know that not being there left a profound emptiness within me. I became very fearful of people dying and leaving me, so much so that I shut my heart off, unable to connect to myself or others.

From that time on, my life was a blank. It was as if my world had collapsed into anxiety attacks, fear, isolation, and pain. I was always the "outsider" - the one that was so sensitive and cried whenever someone brought up the subject of loss. I was caught in a world of my own. Cleverly, I dealt with my acute anxiety and depression with eating. I soon became bulimic, waiting anxiously to fill my belly with food only to violently throw it up. I hated myself afterwards and within hours would repeat the compulsion. It was as if this was my only saving grace, a way to ease my pain from a world that didn't understand who I was, and seemingly wasn't even interested to find out. My Dad knew that I had an eating problem and his reaction was, "You're wasting food!" So I became cleverer and hid it. Though I know others knew my plight, no one spoke up on my behalf.

I left home when I was seventeen. I was just a mere child, desperately wanting to "find my place," yet wanting to return home to my family where I would be nurtured and loved. I sought therapy and quickly learned how easy it was to tell a therapist exactly what she wanted to hear in order to protect my "dark" secrets that were neatly wrapped in shame and guilt and tucked deeply within me. It is amazing how clever we can be, to protect the very secrets that can destroy us.

Because my grief and anxiety were not resolved, I continued to perpetuate the cycle of disconnection and loss of relationships. It's interesting how someone may want to connect with others and say all of the right words, yet the wisdom of the body, which is often referred to as our unconscious, will continue a pattern of operation in order to ensure the survival of the individual. Yet, once that unconscious part of our self becomes conscious, then we can make a change that will ultimately shift our patterns of being.

It has taken me years to come to terms with my sister's death. Not only was she my sister, she was my best friend. From the magical thinking of a child, I was her protector and ultimately was unable to save her from dying. This has been a terrible burden that I have carried, blaming myself, and somehow feeling that I should have been the one to die instead of her. I believe that a part of me wanted to join her, so I gambled with life and took many risks. This was not done on a conscious level; it was the unconscious part of me that felt life was too hard and too sad.

In 2001 my world came crashing down and I desperately sought relief. I went to the Chopra Center and coincidently was there on 9/11, doing my own 911.

My intention for going there was to de-pathologize all of my pathology, the depression, anxiety and addictions. I realized that my so-called disorder was cleverly hiding my grief, trauma and hopelessness. Thus I began my quest to seek out multiple modalities/techniques and approaches of healing myself from the inside out. I attended lots of workshops and trainings. One beloved colleague of mine said to me, "You have attended more workshops than anyone I have ever met." Instead of taking that as an insult, I reframed it and was grateful to that part of myself that was a seeker of resolution and peace.

I now utilize all of my various healing techniques as a useful toolbox for the individuals and groups that I work with. Part of my emotional, mental, physical, and spiritual recovery ultimately was acknowledging what was true in my life. I created rituals to have witnesses help me face my truth. I have learned over the years that though I may not have liked my fate or various life circumstances, they were a reality. Consenting to my truth allowed space to open up and I eventually found deep resolution and peace that led me to my deep healing on a physical, mental, emotional and spiritual level. The war was over, and it was time to honor the warrior who had so gallantly stood up on behalf of my survival. I bow deeply to that part of myself and release her with love.

Healing Heart Tips

I have learned along the way that we are all doing the very best that we can at any given moment in our life. When I can be compassionate and kind it helps to facilitate healing, not only for myself but with others as well.For years I felt ashamed of my sensitivity. Now I have found that it is my gift. What is your greatest gift? The truth can set you free. I invite you to acknowledge what is true in your life and own it. Once you do, it will feel as though a heavy burden has been lifted. I am so grateful that I have come upon so many wonderful mentors, healers, and teachers from all around the world, who have shown me the way to live a more joyful and fulfilling life. It is with tremendous gratitude that I give back to others who may also be suffering the pains of life, and perhaps guide them to find the Light at the end of the tunnel. Our natural state is one of joy. Healing from the inside out enables us to stand tall, regardless of our circumstances.

Catherine VanWetter, MSW is a Holistic Family Healing Practitioner trained in a variety of healing techniques that help people find peace within themselves. She invites you to be gentle, compassionate, and courageous as you put down your weapon of choice and step into a field of Grace. If you are ready to take full responsibility for your life and let go of any story or drama that you are carrying that encumbers your happiness and well-being, visit www.ToTheHeartOfTheMatter.com.

Transformative Power of Intimacy

Philip Belzunce, PhD., N.D., RPE, S/LMFT, CPC

Setting The Scene

"You...you...I am so sorry, you have a muscle cancer," my oncologist friend murmured through his quivering lips. I opened my mouth to react, but my brain was so obliterated by his seeming death sentence that no sound came out.

I had woken up one spring Tuesday morning and seen a "golf-sized ball" bulging out of my left forearm. I was told that one possible cause of this abnormality was the repeated severe traumas inflicted on my arm.

Flashback

Though I had worked very hard to deal with my past traumas, I was not aware that my body was still carrying hidden residues and heavy rusty anchors of my "first" death sentence. "We will kill you, you son-of-a-bitch commie!" One of the high-ranking soldiers was screaming close to my face with relentless intensity. His shrill and evil voice held me captive and powerless. My contorted facial expression betrayed my disbelief at the horror of what was happening to me.

Many years ago I was a young and active Catholic priest in the Philippines. Those were horrible and dangerous times when the country was under martial law. Injustices and killing of innocent Filipinos were rampant under the dictatorial government.

I preached and lectured "revolution" everywhere, including the countryside, conference rooms, and church pulpits. My intention was for the listeners to search inside themselves to transform their fears, which were the product of being victims, to a collective functioning force of courage. My hope was to strengthen and mobilize my countrymen's convictions and revulsion against the injustices being generated by the dictatorial government.

What kind of revolution was I talking about? I was talking about a non-violent kind of revolution...not a bloody massacre! I wanted a revolution of our hearts; a revolution of our minds; and especially a revolution of our souls ..."A revolution that can move mountains!" (p. 32, Belzunce, P., (1999). *Heart Shadows*, Caritas Communications, Wisconsin.)

Like many of my fellow leaders, I was very much influenced by Paulo Freire's Theology of Liberation and the Pedagogy of the Oppressed. The whole message and goal of the theology of liberation was that each individual has to become a free and fully functioning human being. I believed that by liberating ourselves individually and as a nation, we can begin to change the deeply imbedded system of internalized colonialism wherein human beings behaved in oppressing ways towards each other.

That was the horrendous reality in the country that I loved. I suffered immensely as a political prisoner for several months until I found refuge in the United States. I was tortured and most of the time, isolated. In my deep loneliness, passing thoughts of God as a bloodthirsty avenger, rather than the creator of love and forgiveness, tortured my soul. When I allowed myself to dwell on those painful thoughts, my heart ached painfully, and thus immobilized me physically, mentally, and spiritually. I succumbed to deep fear and loneliness. I was in the dark night of my soul.

Begin The Journey

When I was diagnosed with atypical muscle cancer, I was frightened. I had never felt so alone. My loneliness was worse than what I'd felt when I was incarcerated. This time my body became the prison jail. This became my "second" death sentence. I felt overwhelmed and powerless.

Overcoming The Obstacle

My journey to healing started through my friends who comforted and consoled me. There is truth to the old saying that it takes a village to raise a child; and wisdom to the fact that it takes a community of loving friends to support the healing of its wounded members.

It was through the empowering of my community of friends that I gained the energy to participate fully in taking responsibility for managing my healing process. I dug deep inside myself and applied the "revolution of the mind and soul" that I used to preach zealously to others in order to mobilize my inner potency. I changed my diet, meditated and prayed longer, sought natural ways of body/energy healing, and truly discovered the real key to healing and transformation.

The key that opened my heart completely was the recognition that through the healing power of my marriage, I was able to toss away the residual chains that had held me down. I feel truly blessed that I found a woman who was willing to take the journey of unfolding the mystery of marriage with me. I call our relationship a miracle of continuing revolutionary transformative growth of my whole being.

In the depths of my pain, fears, loneliness, and depression our marriage became a transformative healing process. It was in both my unknowing vulnerability and the openness of my wife that our relationship was allowed to deepen and expand.

In the seminary, I had stumbled upon an extremely disturbing man-made rule about celibacy. I discovered that Popes, Bishops and Priests were allowed to marry until the 12th century; that nowhere does the Bible say that priests should be celibate; that most, if not all, of the apostles whom Jesus Christ chose to lead His church had wives; and that St. Peter, the first pope, was married. As I delved more into this subject, I became more enlightened about how the injustice of mandatory celibacy and the self-interests of the powerful held the Eucharist and other sacraments hostage, at the expense of countless suffering and dehumanized individuals.

My marriage to my wife, Lalei, has humanized me. It has increased my love and compassion, which comes from an inner truth, and which cannot be based on any intellectual or philosophical dictum or measured by the thickness of the canon law book. One of my greatest realizations was my unconscious fear of intimacy. I realized that it was easy for me to hide myself behind the cloak of my priesthood. Paradoxically, in deepening the intimacy of our marriage, I learned the true meaning of love.

Though I knew deep down that I was loved and lovable, I needed to be immersed and bathed in intimacy. I needed to experience this intimacy in an unconditional way, and to be reminded and permit myself to reclaim my deep essence, which is that I am lovable. Through intimacy I rediscovered that my essence is free, pure, and beautiful. This inner core is my birthright and the birthright of every human being. But, as most of us experience in our journey to adulthood, especially in a hurting, victimizing environment, this inner being can become hidden, swallowed, enveloped, and obscured. I failed numerous times to recognize my inner beingness because it had become so encased, so wrapped up in the tormenting helplessness and rage from the past.

What I Learned

One of the lessons that I have learned so vividly can be compared to the sun in the sky. Some days, especially in winter, we may see only the dark clouds and believe with conviction in the delusion that the sun is not present. But just because the bright sun is entirely obscured by the dark clouds, it does not mean that the sun is not there shining.

I learned that no amount of preaching for world peace will ultimately create a harmonious humanity if any of us are still divided within. Through self-discovery and healing in body, emotions, mind, and spirit, to fully embrace my soul journey, I have transformed, with forgiveness and love, past fears and pains, to claim the joy I am living in my present and into my future. I am allowing myself to fully embrace a loving world.

In my profession as an integrative psychologist, a holistic life and relations coach, a healing Tao instructor, an energy worker, a naturopath, a diversity consultant, an international trainer, and licensed marriage and family therapist, I have learned to help individuals, couples, and groups to reclaim their own inner self and beauty.

Through experiences of "dying," I learned the value of living. Though my body was threatened, my spirit became alive. I am now in a space of being truly grateful for how my past experiences have transformed how I perceive life. I believe that my gratitude helps me support my clients in a true theology of liberation through the process of integrating body, mind, and spirit.

How To Apply Wisdom To Your Life

I believe my story reflects how we are all uniquely called to transform the world by the forgiving process of healing in body, mind and spirit and by reclaiming our God-like beingness, which we all possess WITHIN. Examine your life experience for opportunities to reclaim yourself through forgiveness and love. Together we can create a powerful tsunami of revolutionizing love that inundates and transforms our world to a world of peace. I believe with deep conviction that even in the darkest nights of our humanity, there is the light of the shining sun.

Oh… by the way, I am fully healed, enjoying fabulous health, and loving the shining light in my life.

Reference:
Belzunce, P., (1999). *Heart Shadows*, Caritas Communications, Mequon, Wisconsin 53092-2010

Philip Belzunce Ph.D., ND, LSMFT, RPE, CPC, is an integrative psychologist, naturopath, life and relationship coach, diversity consultant and author. He derives great satisfaction in serving with a Higher Purpose of facilitating individuals, couples, families and groups through transitions in their life journey and transformations for growth, healing and well-being. To know more of his collaborative work with his wife/partner, go to www.PhilLalei.com and find out how to reconnect with your body-emotion-energy-mind-spirit Life Journey in www.TenPathwaysofHealingLove.com.

Forgiveness - The Key to Unlocking Your Prison

Corinne Ropp

Driving to the courthouse to find out the verdict of my brother's first degree murder trial was like walking into a black hole. My stomach was in knots, I had barely slept the night before, I felt completely numb, and it took all I had to pray that justice would be found inside the courtroom walls.

Arriving in the courtroom with my family members, I felt emotionally paralyzed as I recalled the events of the past four years as if it were a movie replaying itself in my head. Four years of being followed and scrutinized by the police. Four years of people who I thought were my friends and family turning their back on me. Four years of trying to survive despite numerous death threats, personal attacks, and the guilt that perhaps I had not done everything I could have done to protect my brother and my family. Four years of wondering when the next search warrant was going to be executed and when the wire taps were going to be removed. Four years would turn into several more years of trying to find any evidence that would support my brother's innocence.

After going through the metal detector outside the courtroom I could feel the eyes of my sister-in-law's family boring into me, escalating the already high tension in the room to a fever pitch.

Police officers, radiating an aura of disrespect and arrogance, sat in the seats reserved for the family directly behind my brother. As we were escorted to the front row, we politely asked them to move and when they did not do so, the sheriff came and ordered them to vacate their seats. The brashness of the way they used tunnel vision to target my brother would haunt me for some time.

A seventy-two day murder trial ensued with no physical evidence, including the location of her body, proving my brother's guilt, except that my sister-in-law was no longer around. Her car was found abandoned at a bus station. The only evidence was a confession by my brother taken under extreme stress to a group of criminals who were actually police officers. This technique is called the "Mr. Big Sting Operation." My brother felt his life was in danger so he made up a story after many hours of intense interrogation.

To my horror, the judge delivered a guilty verdict of second degree murder.

I can remember my body starting to shake, tears brimming, and the feeling that I was not inside my body. I was powerless and so confused that this could have happened. Anger was at the surface and I wanted revenge. Emotions rushed through me and I could do nothing, so I stuffed them inside, to be dealt with at a later date.

And yet, I knew in my heart that one day my brother would be exonerated, and that this event would have significant meaning for me.

Two years after the verdict, the appeals were not successful. However, one moment in time would start to clear the fog my life had been surrounded in. A mere sixty seconds of time would allow the beginning of my ascension into healing and forgiveness, and become a benchmark in my life. I would open up to a world that had been closed to me for many years - the spirit world.

I was deep in meditation one evening, a practice I had begun using to relax my ever-so-busy mind, when the spirit of my sister-in-law appeared in my mind. It was so real, my heart raced, my breathing grew shallow, and I was quite agitated. It was so intense that even my dog was at the door of the room, scratching and breathing hard, attempting to get my attention.

The conversation I had with her in my mind was about her wanting to connect with someone. She was waiting for me to connect in meditation. She wanted to let me know that my brother did not kill her. We talked about how badly I felt about how I had treated her when she was alive. We were able to have an amazing healing and forgiving conversation. Tears flowed from my eyes as I released the guilt of that relationship and the forgiveness started.

Later that same day I was starting to doubt the encounter and was thinking that I must have made it up in my head because I so desperately wanted to heal my heart of the pain of the whole event. This murder and subsequent trial had become my identity - and the reason for my existence. I could not let the injustice of it go, nor could I forgive anyone involved.

To ensure that I did not let this event slip by, the spirit of my sister-in-law presented itself to both of my daughters and my brother. It was like I was being reminded to accept the spirit experience and learn from it.

That meditation led me to many teachers, including a native spiritual healer who taught me many wonderful things about meditation, intuition, and the spirit world. I was also introduced to hypnotherapy, leadership training, and energy healing.

During that time many events would unfold to make sure that I knew my sister-in-law was around. My daughters and I went to visit my brother in prison where I had picked up a folder from him. As I started to thumb through the file I noticed there was sticky note with my brother's handwriting on it. The quote was from the son that my brother and sister-in-law have. It said, "Mommy's in the dirt," dated April 27, 1994, twenty days after her disappearance. At the same time I was reading this my daughter let out a blood curdling scream from the other end of the house. I ran to her and found her sobbing, pointing to the white linoleum floor. "I just saw my aunt and she told me to tell you that she is in the dirt," she cried. Little tufts of dirt were on the floor, even though it had been cleaned that morning.

The time I get to spend with my brother is precious to me. Five years after he was incarcerated he was diagnosed with a brain tumor and has recovered. He is an inspiration to me and others as he works in the prison chapel, facilitating a course in forgiveness and healing. To be an inspiration to others even when one loses everything is powerful.

I still have no idea where my sister-in-law is and there is no physical evidence to back up my brother's life-threatened confession or the conviction. I have found solace in knowing this event happened for a reason, as all things in life do.

I have discovered that even in the most traumatic experiences, forgiveness can be found through calming the mind by detaching from the emotion. Calming the mind using techniques such as meditation and hypnotherapy can be extremely beneficial.

With meditation, one can understand that calming your thoughts is key to bringing the mind into the now. When you achieve this state you can allow the seed of forgiveness to be planted and to grow.

With hypnotherapy, I was able to resolve the emotional trauma easily without having to relive the event, allowing forgiveness to flow effortlessly.

When I was fearful of being judged, losing my brother, and having my idealistic world turned upside down, I began to understand that these events happened to bring me to my purpose, and every step I took led me here to this moment.

My life is about choosing inspiration as I serve others. When I assist another to achieve their dreams I live my purpose.

As I write this, it is my hope that all people can find inspiration so that they, too, can find peace in the forgiveness of themselves and others. Everyone deserves to find happiness, and forgiveness is the beginning of an incredible journey.

When one reaches a place where the hurt becomes so clear that the only way to find peace is through forgiveness, the simple act of letting go of the habit of the pain of the past will allow you to feel whole again.

True forgiveness for me is to give as before, and when one finds forgiveness, it is the person forgiving that finds peace. When I forgive myself it sets me free—the same happens when I also forgive another.

I now am blessed to be able to walk strong and feel joy in all of life. I find the best teachers are the ones that have gone through what they teach, as forgiveness is not a textbook lesson. I truly believe that life is meant to be lived in complete wholeness and in peace. May you, too, experience the freedom that true forgiveness can bring to your life.

Corinne Ropp is an intuitive spiritual teacher, speaker, and business woman, with a Masters Degree in Behavioral Science. Working in the personal development field gave Corinne the inspiration to create YOU Seminars Inc., a transformational seminar where participants are inspired, through a series of experiences, to empower themselves to live the life of their choosing. To receive a complimentary copy of Unlocking the Seven Keys of Forgiveness, *please visit www.YouSeminars.com/forgiveness.*

Starting Over:
A Journey of Loss
and Recovery

~⁔◯

Margaret Sarkissian

I had not planned to reinvent myself at the age of sixty, but life had its own plans for me. So, instead of spending the day dealing with human rights complaints, I am sitting here in my neighborhood café, writing my book, and preparing for my upcoming workshop. But I am getting ahead of myself. Here's how I journeyed from loss to recovery, building my life as a writer, coach, teacher, and healer at sixty.

Until two years ago, my whole career involved working for a large non-profit organization. I started as a young university graduate in the Personnel department. Over time I worked in many different areas, and eventually was promoted to senior human rights advisor dealing with discrimination and harassment complaints. While I was skillful at this, I most enjoyed teaching workshops on human rights issues such as anti-racism, preventing sexual harassment, accommodating disability and valuing diversity. I had a reputation in the organization as compassionate and fair in handling human rights complaints, and knowledge-able and engaging as a trainer.

While my organization had a policy prohibiting workplace discrimination and harassment, it had not yet developed a policy addressing bullying, and unfortunately, bullying seemed to be on the rise. This was a widespread phenomenon; other large organizations were also reporting increased complaints of bullying and had the same limited toolkit for handling them. One particular case stands out from the many I handled. An intelligent, articulate woman in her early forties, whom I will call Alison, came to my office at first asking for information related to her disability benefits. She soon, however, began to tell me about being bullied by her manager, and enduring it for months, until collapsing into a major depression. She was now on sick leave and although in therapy, was still barely able to look after her most basic needs. As she talked she became more and more agitated and anxious, soon crying with such intensity and despair that I felt alarmed. As a counselor, I could see that there was a very real possibility of her harming herself, especially if she were pressured to return to the work environment that had made her ill. It was obvious that she would need considerable time to recover her emotional and physical health. It was also obvious to me that she could *not* recover as long as she knew that she had to return to the unit in which she had been bullied.

This case was a turning point for me. Alison had tried to report the bullying, but as was often the case, had no evidence or witnesses to support her complaint. Because her manager was so senior, and because there was no evidence, I knew there was little I could do to assist her. She was now in the situation of having to return to the very environment that had made her ill.

I realized that there would always be cases like this, *people* like this who were being brutalized by bullying, for whom there would be no true remedy. I began to yearn for different work - work that *prevented* bullying and the other workplace ills that I saw daily which caused people such pain. In addition I was experiencing significant concerns in my own unit about our new director's mode of management, and was asking myself whether I was willing to spend the last years of my career under this leadership style. So, I returned to school and completed a graduate certificate in executive coaching, hoping that this would open new doors for me, although I could not imagine what those doors might be.

I was thinking only to make a small change, a *careful* change, perhaps working part-time in my job while building my coaching practice. I was afraid to make the *big* change and leave my job. I was fifty-eight, making a good salary, and still supporting my son at university. I told myself that I could have a small coaching practice on the side and that would have to suffice until I could afford to leave the workforce for good. But I was wrong. The Universe had other plans for me. Within two weeks of graduating from my coaching program, we hired a new staff person I'll call Alex, setting in motion a series of events that blew my world apart.

Though I could see that our director, whom I'll call Morgan, was knowledgeable in human rights, I could not help but see a corresponding lack in other important skills. Unwisely and unprofessionally, I confided to Alex some of my frustrations. Alex promptly told Morgan, which, of course, destroyed our already tenuous working relationship. Although I apologized, irreparable harm was done. Needless to say, I carefully avoided Alex from then on. I was stunned, therefore, when Morgan continued to bring forward allegations on a weekly basis. These new allegations were untrue, and in some instances even bizarre, but the die was cast. Morgan believed them. As these allegations mounted up, my anxiety soared. I could not believe this was happening. I had spent thirty-three years with this organization and had exemplary performance reviews, while Alex had worked there two months and was still on probation. I began to see that I was in a negative spiral from which I could not save myself. My anxiety reached an all-time high, and I started to have difficulties concentrating, then sleeping, then eating, and finally could barely cope at all.

I went to an advisor in Human Resources for help, but could barely speak, as I was so distraught. The advisor explained to me that Human Resources would manage the situation from this point on; all weekly meetings would be suspended while she reviewed the facts. She further explained that I could not be fired for complaining about my director, especially since I had apologized. Since I was so incapacitated with anxiety, she approved an immediate medical leave. Within a few days the advisor contacted me at home offering me a new position elsewhere in the organization, but I was too unwell to even consider the offer. The irony of this was not lost on me. I had become my client Alison - too fragile to even *think* about returning to work. I came to the painful realization that my career there was over. This was a devastating heartbreak as the organization had been my home, my community for my whole adult life. I had many close friends and a wide network of colleagues, but it was clear to me that this part of my life was now over.

Recovering from this loss took a full year. I plunged into a deep depression, feeling that I had lost my identity, my path, my future. Yet in the back of my mind I also *knew* that I had made the right decision, the *only* decision, when I refused my previous employer's offer of another job. Somehow I knew I was meant to leave the organization and comfortable career, in order to pursue the work I had always longed to do – writing, coaching, teaching, and healing.

My family, close friends and health care team helped me immeasurably, and carried me through some of the darkest times. With their support, I was able to say "*yes*" to the loss, "*yes*" to the unknown, and "*yes*" to Spirit. In return, I felt the hand of the Universe holding me, guiding me back to my true self - the self that I had put on hold for so many years. Although I did not know how I *could* start over at my age, I trusted that I could, and would, and that somehow, although I could not see it, my future was shaping itself as I healed. Throughout all this the Universe miraculously kept bringing me money whenever I most needed it.

Gradually, I rebuilt my life, inviting in only those elements that passed my new truth test: Is this *heart-based* work? And only if the answer were positive did I say "yes." So, now I am coaching again, and facilitating a course on living joyfully, based on the book, "The Joy of Appreciative Living," by Jacqueline Kelm. I am co-teaching a coaching skills workshop with a former colleague back at my old organization, and am writing a book on building healthy workplaces. I am learning advanced techniques in alternative healing, building that practice, and am birthing new ideas and opportunities for heart-based work all the time.

I awake each morning with a sense of peace. I make my daily gratitude list, especially appreciating the time and freedom that I now have to do what I always dreamed of. I view my former director as a catalyst for my life-giving transformation, freeing me from work I had outgrown and an unhappy environment that was deadening my soul. The perfect storm that appeared to be demolishing my life was, in fact, a gift from the Universe that has led me to the most creative and meaningful work of my entire life.

Margaret Sarkissian, M.A. (Counseling Psychology), Certified Coach, is a skilled consultant, trainer, and business/life coach. She has worked with 200+ managers, helping them address serious workplace problems, and has extensive experience facilitating workshops on coaching and communication skills, diversity and inclusion, building respectful workplaces, strategic planning, and appreciative living. If you are experiencing workplace problems and/or want to determine whether coaching would help with your personal or work goals, go to www.ClearPerspectives.ca.

Awakening to Her True Self

Colleen Russell

"She who would find a new land, must lose sight of the shore for a very long time."

- SOURCE UNKNOWN

The blades of the life flight helicopter echoed loudly off the walls of the Sunrise Ski Lodge at Mount Bachelor outside of Bend, Oregon. I watched as it took flight and disappeared from sight. My husband Dennis was inside.

When we got into the car, my seventeen year old son tried to convince me that Dennis was still alive. "He's alive, Mom. I know he is alive! I watched them give him an electric shock." Even though a part of me wanted to believe him, my instincts told me differently.

My brother-in-law drove us down the mountain. When we arrived at the hospital there was a man waiting at the door. He said, "I want you to know your husband is dead. I'm sorry."

My head swirled. I thought I was going to vomit. That morning we'd been skiing, enjoying the warmth of a beautiful sunny day. It had been the perfect way to spend Christmas Eve. We'd driven over before daybreak from Sandy, Oregon, to spend the holidays with family. Now I was sitting in a hospital calling Dennis' family to inform them he was dead of a heart attack.

When we arrived at my sister's house, the rest of my family had arrived. The smell of roasted turkey filled the air. The dinner was nearly done, but no one knew what to do. "Do we open the presents...or what?" asked my eldest sister. The flow of life hadn't stopped because Dennis had died. The little ones still expected Christmas. We continued with the festivities.

Four days passed before we could return home. When I got out of the car in front of our house, the impact of walking through the door without Dennis hit me like a lightening bolt. I fell to the ground sobbing.

Inside, reminders were everywhere of our last morning together. Dennis' empty coffee cup sat on the counter and the newspaper still lay open on the table. Everything was the same and yet nothing was. I didn't know how I'd ever put my life back together.

I thought I might find refuge when I returned to work, but I felt like a stranger as people passed by in silence or fumbled through condolences. I didn't feel like I belonged anywhere.

I was in the world, but not in it. I had begun what I would later come to know as an archetypal journey. Grief became the portal for me to find my true self. At the time of Dennis's death, I was thirty-five. He was forty-seven. We had been married for five years and I had been a single mom before then.

In the beginning stages of grief, I felt like a lost child who was confused, lonely, and scared. I felt abandoned, a feeling I had experienced often in childhood. Gratefully I already had a guide in place so I didn't have to take the journey alone.

I had seen Sherry, my counselor, a couple of times before Dennis's death, because I was feeling depressed. She now encouraged me to embrace my grief, not to run from it. For the first six months, she held me as I cried. She validated my feelings, assured me I wasn't going crazy and that I could trust myself. She encouraged me to hit my anger out on pillows, anger I didn't even know I had.

She was there for me when Matthew graduated from high school six months later and moved out on his own. She said he needed to take his own journey and that I shouldn't make him feel like he needed to take care of me. When I found out he was taking acid, she guided me through that too. She taught me how to support him without taking his power away. He was relieved to have support. As I look back now, I see she was a very wise woman.

She talked me into attending a co-dependency group that she and her husband were offering. There I learned to identify and reclaim some of the power I had lost in childhood. I experienced how wounded my inner child was and how important it was that I not abandon her now. Sherry introduced me to the importance of women finding their true power. She had hopes I would find my true self.

After a year and a half of working with Sherry, she recommended that I give up my job. She said I was like a cup that was overflowing and that if I was going to get through this, I needed to let go, to make space for something new to be born. So I gave up my seven-year sales career at the Yellow Pages and my work with her.

Now no longer an employee, I found myself separated from my work community too. At first, I felt guilty about leaving, and then angry with Sherry as I felt the pangs of more loss. Thankfully the grief no longer consumed me. New life was beckoning.

A few months later, I put all of my household goods into storage and traveled to the British Isles to explore my Irish ancestry. I began my explorations at the Findhorn Foundation, a spiritual community in

Scotland. Daily we met for groups, danced, and worked in the gardens. I noticed that no matter where people came from, they still had a deep longing to know God and themselves.

From Findhorn I traveled to the Island of Iona to attend a workshop called Birthing the Undivided Self. There in a little cottage overlooking the sea, while rain and wind battered our windows, several of us explored what it meant to birth our undivided selves. We learned that birth and death always overlap in creation. We had to empty before something new could be born.

A friend met me a couple of weeks later in London and we traveled together, parting in Ireland. I went to stay with Packy and Lizzie, the elderly couple who now owned my grandmother's land. Every night Packy shared stories, as we sat in front of the peat fire, about how life had been before the great immigration. He had been a child when my grandmother had left for America.

Later I returned to Iona to begin a month of solitude and writing. Jane, one of the grandmothers of the Island, rented me a cottage. It sat in a field surrounded by a white picket fence overlooking the crystal clear water below.

Jane had lost her husband a year before and had a son about my son's age. That bond drew us together. She invited me often for tea. She said she hadn't grieved much after her husband had died from cancer. Instead, she'd taken buckets of water and scrubbed the barn floor over and over for several days on her hands and knees.

As the days passed, I felt ready to step back into life. It became clear to me that I could help others through major life transitions. My experience could become my gift. My time on the Island had been healing.

The morning I was to catch the ferry back to London and then return home, a rainbow appeared. Jane said it was a sign I would return some day. To date I have not returned, but I still write to her every Christmas. (Sadly, a few years after my departure, Jane's son and several of the other young men from the island drowned on their way home from a dance. Their loss was greatly mourned.)

When I came back to the states I moved to Bend, Oregon, the town where Dennis had died. New feelings of grief resurfaced. I was alone again without an identity.

I knew finding a job would help. I began teaching classes on change and transition through the community college and pursued a Master's degree in Transpersonal Psychology. I specialized in spiritual crisis, (as a pathway to transformation), creativity, and women's studies. It became an empowering three-year period of personal and spiritual growth.

While living in Bend, I met a wise and loving man who had been through his own dark night of the soul. It was scary and challenging to open my heart again. Randy and I married in 1996, and together designed and created an emotional growth and leadership school for young adults in transition.

It's now been eighteen years since Dennis' death and I continue to grow and evolve. My creativity has blossomed. Even though it was painful, I feel happier and more alive now than ever.

If you find yourself in a difficult transition, take a deep breath. Recognize that you are on a sacred journey. Find support from someone who has been through a deep initiatory experience. Grieve for what was and follow your intuition. Let it lead you to your soul's path. Surrender to the mystery and trust.

Colleen Russell, *co-owner of www.SouLore.com, combines nature aware-
ness, Native American Spirituality, and the creative and expressive arts to
help both young and old discover their authentic selves. They transform lives
and the world by awakening people to their inner and outer nature. To sign up
for Colleen's e-zine and Free report, visit www.Quest4Wholeness.com. Colleen
is available for speaking, workshops, and private coaching. Check her website
for upcoming women's retreats.*

From Trauma to Triumph: One Woman's Conscious Empowering Journey from Fragmented Child to Conscious Entrepreneur

Charlon Bobo

At nine years old, I was molested by a trusted female caregiver. For reasons of mental self-preservation, I carried the knowledge -- neatly nestled, details hidden from my full awareness -- for the next twenty-five years.

I don't remember the impetus for deciding that at age thirty-four I was ready to know the details. I guess it had to do with having support. I was in a safe relationship and I knew no matter what unfolded, I would not be walking this path alone. As it turned out, I didn't need more than a silent witness to my process.

I said aloud, "I am ready to know the specifics and in the next week, they will come to me." With confidence, I knew I would have the tools when I needed them, although in the moment I had no idea what or how this would unfold.

As I intended, within the week, in my mind's eye and in vivid color, I saw exactly what had happened. It was the middle of the night and I bolted straight up in bed. I said to my husband, "I know what happened." I described the scene to him and listened to the story myself as if it were someone else's experience.

I was looking down on my tiny nine year old body. I was on my back on the floor of the kitchen area of an after school daycare facility. A woman's fingers were inside me. I saw the glassy eyes of that nine year old child whose tiny hands were holding up her dress. In her lack of understanding, this action meant she had granted the woman permission. How misguided that little girl was. Her eyes were dead. She had gone to another place in her mind; a place where she was safe.

I knew in this pivotal moment that the decisions I would make in the next minutes, combined with this knowing, would to some degree determine my mental wellness for the rest of my life. I had to quickly decide what I wanted to do with knowing the details.

Mentally, as the adult Charlon, I walked into the kitchen where the molestation was taking place and I took the child's hand in mine. I talked to her and said, "It wasn't your fault. Nothing like this will happen again. I have come back for you."

I took her outside into the sunshine, as its shining brilliance symbolized the room of my mind that had been inaccessible and shrouded in darkness for so long. I invited in the sunlight so I could see there was nothing there to cause more pain.

Now it was time to decide. I said aloud, "It happened. That I cannot change. What I have power over in this moment is deciding what I want to do now. I am determined that this experience will not be meaningless and wasted. I consciously choose that this experience will serve me and others." Being a victim was not an option.

I had to decide what I would do about the person who set this experience in motion. In an instant I made my decision. In order to live at peace with myself, I had to sever my ties with her. I said, "I now release her to her own fate based on the decisions she made." That was the extent of my need to address her.

I had never felt such peace. I knew I had finally taken care of the business that had been patiently waiting to be settled for twenty-five years. Awash in relief, resolve, clarity, and a newfound empowerment, I allowed every emotion to flow through me.

With my husband serving as a silent witness, I released the vastness of emotion that had had no outlet until this very moment. I began crying out in anger for the child whose sexuality was accessed without tenderness, compassion, or permission. I mourned deeply for the child who couldn't understand why no one had protected her. I sobbed for the child who had assumed full responsibility for being molested and didn't know the responsibility rested with everyone but her.

I cried out with a sound that I'd never made or heard before. It was a primal scream of torment. A combination scream/cry/screech that permeated the room, the house, and the neighborhood. Momentarily, I was afraid of that sound. It echoed into the ether.

My cries were heard.

Held preciously in the hand of the Universe, a wounded soulful creature's distress was being transformed. Alongside the pain paralleled something miraculous and indefinable. There was indeed something sweet waiting for me on the other side of this journey.

There I was. All I could do was sit with it, to sit with myself, directly facing everything that had happened, and face it with a courage that I did not know I possessed. In the moment, it didn't feel like courage, yet I knew it was the only thing I could do if I wanted to be free.

Now that I was in it, I was going to shine the light in every corner, every crevice. NOTHING would go unseen. Until that task was finished, I sat. And sat. I have no idea how much time passed.

In the end, with tears still streaming down my cheeks, soaking my nightshirt and pooling in my lap, I laid my head on the pillow and fell into the most blissful sleep of my life.

When I awoke, it felt like a dream. But it was so much more than that. I had faced my deepest, darkest fear… **that I wouldn't be able to manage so much pain if all of it was in front of me at one time.**

I was wrong.

I was wrong for all those years.

Not only did I willingly and bravely step into the seemingly bottomless well of pain with courage, I also took back what was rightfully mine all along - my birthright. To be whole and complete, fully-integrated, with nothing to hide, from myself or anyone else. After all, I was a child.

Now, as an adult, I was truly free.

The Final Outcome

Since that fateful, blessed night, now so many years ago, the experience of recapturing my power - and the resulting freedom - flows gently and gracefully into every area of life. I thrive because I know nothing can take from me what I've intentionally and boldly reclaimed as my own.

As strange as it even seems to me at times, the lessons of my childhood journey are applicable to every aspect of my life, including the everyday operations of my soulful business. As a conscious entrepreneur, I pull from this experience often to guide me. I'd like to share with you the five key lessons of my pilgrimage.

- **Protective mechanisms are in place whether or not I realize or acknowledge them.** I don't always understand why a project fails to materialize or a serious prospect seems to change her mind. I do know there exists an over-arching structure and order that conspires on my behalf to bring about my highest personal and professional growth. Whatever that wisdom, I can trust it absolutely.

- **My "story" doesn't define who I am.** I am a vibrant business owner who grows every day, and occasionally stumbles and falls on my bum! Because I constantly create myself anew, nothing from my past can effectively define or imprison me. I consciously choose to "bring my best game" to every day and know that's enough.

- **Innate wisdom effortlessly guides me to the most opportune time to take action.** When in doubt, I do nothing until ultimate clarity presents itself. Although daily action is a crucial component in accomplishing my goals, I can also watch nature and use Her guidance to positively influence my actions. Nature provides a silent, fallow season – winter – to turn inward to rest and restore. Using this model, I reap the most benefit from my efforts. Smart living requires me to balance action with equal inaction.

- **My history doesn't determine my level of success.** I can accomplish any lofty goal I imagine regardless of any perceived limitations. The past doesn't dictate my future. I gift myself the pleasure and freedom to envision a life of my design. Family-of-origin, childhood circumstances, real or perceived impediments, lack of skills, none of these compare to the capacity of the human spirit to realize dreams.

- **I choose victimhood or empowerment every day with my words, thoughts, and actions.** We do not control the actions of others and yet we may be drawn into their drama. Like cast members of a play, energetically we agreed to these roles to teach AND learn. No matter my external circumstances, my responses can only come from one of two places: damage or abundance. I choose abundance.

May you be profoundly blessed by reading my story and take from it any value that forever nourishes your soul.

Charlon Bobo *is the visionary behind EditCopyProof. Affectionately known as the "conscious copywriter," she provides wordsmithing solutions for conscious entrepreneurs. EditCopyProof is the single and final destination in your quest for copywriting, editing and proofreading services that effectively communicate with your heart-centered audience. Increase your sales, credibility, and exposure based on your genuine desire to connect, serve or create community. To receive your complimentary report* The 7 Elemental Facets of Heart-focused Copywriting *visit www.EditCopyProof.com and www.CharlonBobo.com.*

Let God Do
the Driving

~~◯)

Jan Janzen

It was Labor Day 2000 and as my husband of eighteen years packed to move out, it was the closest thing to actual labor I'd ever felt. My tears flowed like Niagara Falls. I felt like my heart had been cut out of my chest, cut in little pieces, and handed back to me on a chopping board. There were no words to describe the utter feeling of loneliness, fear, and despair I was experiencing.

It had only been a year before that we had made a joint decision to leave the Jehovah's Witnesses church where we had spent the first thirty-eight years of our lives. With that one decision, we had already lost all of our friends and most of our family. Now my soul mate, the man I had vowed to live with forever, had his suitcases packed and was headed out the door.

Just a couple of months later, my primary customer, Ford Canada, made an executive decision that wiped out 80% of my business. Now, I was not only alone, I was facing financial ruin. Being alone looked even scarier than just a few months before.

Things did go from bad to worse and within a period of about eighteen months, I had gone from being happily married, earning a six-figure income and living in a beautiful home overlooking the ocean, to being almost bankrupt, homeless, and divorced.

On top of that, the solace I had found for my entire life in a faith that was once as strong as the Rock of Gibraltar, had sunk like the Titanic when we left the regime and structure of our religious organization. I didn't do the "G" word anymore. I didn't want to hear about God and I certainly wasn't willing to look to God to fix any of my problems. I honestly felt like God had caused many of them.

But then the problems became so immense, overwhelming, and terrifying, that one day I flung myself on my bed sobbing and once again connected with God. This was no "Our Father" prayer. It was a prayer of anger, fear, and despair, but boy, did it feel good to be talking with Him again!

Life didn't turn around overnight. It didn't even turn around for a while. I was starting from scratch, exploring a whole new life - a brand new way of being, and it didn't come easily. One day a friend looked at me and said, "Jan, your outer world is a reflection of your inner world." I looked at her with tears in my eyes and felt nausea overwhelm me at the immensity of transforming my inner world. I had been in a blender of emotions, conflicts, and struggles since leaving my religion. There was no foundation, no touchstone any longer; there was no one to turn to.

However, over the next couple of years, my relationship with a Higher Power strengthened. I started ministerial training and pummeled my teacher with questions. I was a disruptive student, an inquisitive learner, and hard to satisfy. I needed answers and I needed them fast. I was hard on God too. I had little patience, no time to waste, and a list of questions a mile long that I demanded answers to.

Through this all, friends came and went, as I was too unstable, volatile, and self-absorbed to be fully present for anyone. My whole world needed to revolve around me because the upheaval going on inside was creating tidal waves everywhere I turned. Business wasn't going well, my finances were still in the toilet, and my relationships were tumultuous. My ex-husband was getting remarried. My health was suffering. And I had no one but God to turn to.

I kept on remembering the scripture, "Draw close to God, and He will draw close to you." Well, God was stuck with me because I was like a barnacle on a ship. However, I wasn't going to be a docile, obedient servant. I was interested in a partnership and a 50/50 one at that. I'd do the work, but I was committed to the idea that I would be supported.

Support didn't always look like I thought it should. I had asked God to find me an isolated cabin in a forest on the ocean to live in so I could find solace and healing in my home environment. The cabin was handed to me, practically on a silver platter, but along with the oceanfront view surrounded by the forest came the rats running up and down the walls and no heat. One morning my toilet water was frozen, my fridge door wouldn't open because of the ice build up, and I had $100 to my name, no credit rating, and no one to turn to... except God.

We had a feisty conversation that day. It was around that time that Monique came into my life and turned me upside down. She said, "Jan, if you knew what you were doing, your life would be working. Maybe you need to get down on your knees and actually tell God that you don't have a clue, you will surrender and let go of your need to control." The words hit hard and for a few minutes I felt the hair on the back of my neck rise in anger. How dare she talk to me that way! However, she was absolutely right. For all of my "surrender," I had just become a backseat driver. I hadn't surrendered at all. I still was very much in control of my life.

That night I did what Monique told me to do and the tears flowed again. This time I finally gave up and gave over to the wisdom, the support, and the love of the Universe. I felt a wave of peace flow through me as I agreed to let God lead my life.

Within a few short months, I was back on my feet in an entirely new business that prospered. I moved into a beautiful two bedroom condo with a magnificent view of the forest from every window. And although my mother died the Labor Day weekend while I was moving into my new home, I had come a long way in five years since the other long ago Labor Day when my husband had left. I spent every weekend hanging out with God that year. We had some great dates and my confidence grew, my business flourished and my bank account prospered.

A wonderful man came into my life eighteen months later who has loved me unconditionally every minute of our relationship. Friends who had left returned and have become very dear to me. Monique, the woman who had spoken to me so forthrightly, has been my earth angel of wisdom and support. I have been able to live the life of my dreams, living in Mexico for much of the last year and a half.

Did it happen overnight? No, it certainly didn't. But it did happen. Even in the darkest hours, I believed it could.

If you're feeling like you are unsupported, have been abandoned, and are in a place of despair, remember that "prayer" doesn't have to look pretty, sound good or follow a ritual. It can be down and ugly. Surely God understands that we don't always feel like dressing up for the party. Sometimes we need to be in faded jeans and an old sweatshirt. And that's good enough. What loving parent wouldn't want their child to just tell them what was in their heart, even if it wasn't nice or what they wanted to hear? Don't underestimate the love and compassion the Universe has for us!

Secondly, remember that others who have been down and out have transformed their lives, so if they can do it, so can you. Be inspired by others' examples and stories. Know that you too have the capacity within you to do what it takes to move through the challenges. It may be buried in the tip of your toes, but it's there, because you are divine, you are powerful, and you are supported. Feel that love, demand that support, and believe in yourself and what God can do with you.

Thirdly, focus with incredible gratitude on all of the good things that you do have in your life. You may not have new shoes to wear, but do you have feet to walk on? You may not have money in the bank, but do you have freedom to earn the money? You may not have someone to love in your life right now, but do you get that you are loved?

Fourthly, expect to receive. Stop this nonsense of, "I hope I can have…" or "Maybe one day I'll be…" Know beyond a shadow of a doubt that you can have the life you say you want. You wouldn't have the desires to improve your life if you weren't able to achieve them. Trust that, know that, and act as if it's absolutely true. Because… it really is.

Jan Janzen is a non-denominational minister, healer, and business coach. She is the author of Devil with a Briefcase: 101 Success Secrets for the Spiritual Entrepreneur *and* Getting Off the Merry-Go-Round: How to Create the Life You Want Without the Fear, Doubt and Guilt. *She has CDs for the spiritual entrepreneur on how to heal money and weight issues. To receive Jan's complimentary ebook,* 10 Secrets to Living the Life of Your Dreams, *visit www.JanJanzenDaily.com.*

Do you have a book inside you?

Most people do.

LoveYourLife

Love Your Life Publishing, Inc. offers a variety of educational and publishing services especially for the entrepreneurial author who wants to write a book to share wisdom and build a business. We specialize in non-fiction books with a positive message.

Whether you'd like to be considered for our next anthology project, want to learn how to write a full length book in our award-winning Get Your Book Done® program, or have a manuscript ready for publication, Love Your Life Publishing has resources to help you.

If you feel called to share your wisdom in a book, go to www.FreeBookResources.com and download the information there. You'll gain solid information that will help you get started and show you what's possible when you have a book.

You'll also enjoy the free articles, videos, and audios on our website:
www.LoveYourLifePublishing.com

Consider us Your Friends in the Book Business!

Love Your Life Publishing Inc.
7127 Mexico Road, Suite 121
St. Peters, MO 63346
800-930-3713